CALL OF THE RUNNING TIDE

MARION CARR

Call of the Running Tide

FOREWORD
BY
JANE BENHAM

1848

MALDON
AT THE WAVE HOUSE

SAILTRUST LIMITED, Publishers
PO Box 347
Maldon, Essex
CM9 7UZ

British Library Cataloguing in
Publication Data:

Carr, Marion
    Call of the running tide.
    1. Sailing barges — England — History — 20th century
    I. Title   II. Benham, Jane
    387.5'092'4   VM466.B3

ISBN 0-946547-01-7

Printed in Great Britain by
Anchor Brendon Ltd
Tiptree, Essex

Contents

ILLUSTRATIONS

In one or two cases the ascription does not indicate the original photographer, but the present owner of the print used.

ACKNOWLEDGEMENTS

Most of the beautiful photographs reproduced in this book have been lent to me by kind acquaintances. I am deeply grateful for so many pleasant reminders of a happy period of my life, now so far behind me.

I am no kind of historian: only a few snippets of knowledge concerning the earlier adventures of my three barges have chanced my way, for I have no inclination to research. The reader must kindly bear with me in my vaguer moments. However, to rescue me from the total scorn of more inquiring minds, Miss O'Driscoll who is so well known in maritime historical circles, and Mr Henry Higgs between them have supplied me with a little of the history of the three vessels in which I served. This I have assimilated with relish, and it will be found (in my own words) at the end of the narrative.

Miss Jane Benham has been kind enough to read the manuscript and correct where necessary. Her own interesting career on the water began as mine was ending; she has been able to bring some of my recollections of the Thames Estuary into sharper focus.

Finally, I must admit that this is a story I intended never to write. Only the persistence of an old friend (now my publisher) has overcome my native reticence. It has been (I must admit to him) enormous fun re-living those wonderful hours of youth, when my daily habits were ruled by the complexion of the sky, the humour of the weather-glass, and the abstruse calculus of the nautical almanac.

M.C.

Foreword

by

JANE BENHAM

FROM the typewriter of a quiet middle-aged civil servant come exciting tales of her early life when she ran away to sea.

Not to be a lady dinghy-sailing instructor, or stewardess on a cruise liner; she did not go ocean yacht racing under the eye of a cockpit camera nor as supernumerary aboard a replica traditional ship on pleasure bent. Marion Carr answered an advertisement for a mate/cook on a small coasting vessel in the 1950s. It proved to be a Thames sailing barge, the *Clara*. Her father foretold she would be home within weeks. She was to stay at work afloat for the next fourteen years. During those years Miss Carr saw diesel power remove most of the romance and much of the very hard work from the coasting trade. But even in a motor barge there was to be no lack of adventure.

Now, in the 1980s, the remaining Thames sailing barges attract an enormous amount of interest. Marion Carr has not followed their recent fortunes nor delved into the minute details of their early past. As her story goes to press, she is not to be found among today's barge enthusiasts in East Coast pubs, nor does she plan a comeback one Barge Race day to show the "amateurs" how the professionals sailed a barge in trading days.

No, she will be far away, bicycling home across the Welsh border after her Early Music evening class, a treble recorder tucked alongside her sandwich box. Perhaps she is smiling secretly to herself, knowing that her fellow musicians and her civil service colleagues little dream of her adventures with the Irish mice, her triumph with a certain sulky motor-pump, or her shameful part in the affair of the little frozen lamb (she helped to *eat* it).

Here, refreshingly, is a book about the ever-popular Thames sailing barges which has no pretensions to being of the "train-spotters' handbook" type. Names are not dropped; opinions on technical detail are not proffered to appeal to a small band of East Coast *cognoscenti*. This is a book of far wider appeal, and no pretensions to grandeur. It

succeeds as an outstandingly unassuming narrative about a way of life
now vanished. For Marion and her skipper the daily task was to scratch
a living for themselves and their ship: the method was to work
extremely hard, suffer often cold, discomfort and disappointing
weather. Tides ruled their daily routine, and the freight rates were
more important to them than their picturesque appearance.
Sometimes they loaded dangerously deep; often they were close to
peril.

Amusement was seldom absent in the irrepressible (often pawky)
humour of the skipper; occasionally the benevolent hand of fate (or a
friendly docker) brought them the delight of some free tit-bit for an
austere grub locker; on one notable occasion the dull round of river
work was enlivened (for both were voracious readers) when they found
their barge tied up alongside a Thames lighter deep-loaded with old
books. . . .

Those of us today who ply the short-sea-routes Miss Carr remembers
so well cannot help but feel a twinge of envy, for our voyaging, unlike
hers, is precise and pre-set. "To Woolwich for orders. . . ." Orders that
may come tomorrow — or next week; orders for Newcastle or some tiny
inlet on the Cornish coast; orders for Ipswich or Norwich or Maldon:
coal, china clay, cement, wheat from Canada, big logs from Africa,
sand from the River Colne — all of that, and a hop ashore at Rochester
for the evening paper or Gravesend for a bottle of milk. . . .

I Run Away to Sea

THE Europe adventure ought to have cured me of my restlessness. But it didn't. The ignominious way I had come home should have made me content with suburban life in drab post-war Britain. But it hadn't. In 1950 I had spent six months roving about the Continent: northern France, Belgium and Holland, hitching lifts in whatever direction the traffic was heading, occasionally stopping off for a few weeks doing kitchen work at some hotel to earn a little money, finally arriving in Zurich, tired, hungry, covered in dust and quite penniless. When ready to call it a day, and having been conveyed to England from Zurich by courtesy of His Majesty's Government as a Distressed British Subject, I returned to my family home in a London suburb, defiant and not nearly as ashamed as I should have been for causing my long-suffering parents distress and worry. It says much for their forbearance that they allowed me without comment or criticism to return to the run-down little flat where they lived in the cold austerity of post-war England. I picked up my life more or less where I dropped it, except that instead of travelling into Central London every day to work I found a job as a secretary in a local factory which made telephones.

The novelty of my new job wore off after only a few months, and I began to search the columns of Situations Vacant in the *Evening News*. Night after night I pored over the fine print, never quite knowing what to look for, but feeling sure I'd recognise it when I spotted it. Once I applied (it seems odd now, in view of recent history) for a post as secretary somewhere in the Falkland Islands, but I didn't even get an acknowledgement. Then one evening I saw an advertisement which ran something like this:

> "WANTED: female mate/cook for small coasting
> vessel, no experience necessary. Apply Box. . . . ."

At last, this was it! I wrote off immediately, one of seventy-four applicants as I was later told. After a little while I received a letter offering me the job and saying if I wanted it I was to go to a timber wharf in Essex at a certain time where I should find my ship, a sailing barge named *Clara*.

I had never heard of such a thing as a sailing barge and had no idea what it could be. Nevertheless, I gave my employer a week's notice and then broke the news to my parents. My father was most put out and told me that a bargeman was lower than a street sweeper, and I'd certainly not stick it for more than six weeks. In that last dig I saw a serious challenge and in the spirit of: "I'll show him!" I set off for Maldon, determined to make a success of my new job. The moment I set my eyes on that extraordinary vessel, the sailing barge *Clara,* I knew that this was going to be *some* adventure.

The only ships I'd ever been aboard in my life were H.M.S. *Hood* when she had an open day off Southend-on-Sea, before the war — and the only thing I remember about that visit was being handed a slab of Swiss roll by the cook somewhere in the bowels of the ship: I had also sailed twice in cross-Channel ferries.

As far as sea-faring ancestors are concerned, all I know is that my father was an apprentice radio officer in the Royal Navy just before the First World War. He had left after discovering that he wasn't amenable to naval discipline. My mother, after emigrating from Tyneside to London as a young woman, used to travel back and forth between London and the Tyne by way of passenger-carrying cargo ships, mainly because it was cheap, but also because she liked travelling by water!

I had learned to row a small boat when very young, and I could swim like a fish, so that was something to start off with.

When I got aboard and found the ship deserted I poked about, found where companion ladders led to, and tried to make some sense of the bewildering tangle of ropes that festooned the lofty masts, wondering where the engine was hidden. The skipper came aboard some time later and we introduced ourselves. I helped him cover up the cargo hold and pull the heavy tarpaulins over. Then he did mysterious things with the sails. Some men on the quay let go our ropes. We drifted off down the river. It was late in the afternoon, and November time — calm and clear with a light breeze from the West which increased after nightfall. The picture is for ever vivid in my mind. The sun low behind Maldon Hill, a clear pale sky, flushed pink; the calm water. The barge with topsail set and part of the mainsail loosened, ghosting down past moored yachts and fising boats, out into the wider reaches at Heybridge, then on past Osea Island where the land began to disappear in the gathering darkness. We lit the regulation red and green lamps and put them in the rigging. I don't remember much about that night's passage but the breeze must have been sufficient to see us into an anchorage off Kent before morning.

This then was my first practical experience afloat. I learned my new work as the *Clara* went on about her business. I found out from day to day as we sailed up the Thames how ropes and sails and leeboards worked. We loaded timber in the Surrey Docks, and wheat in the South West India; we took beans (the kind that get baked into tins) out of a ship in Tilbury to Whitstable where a thoughtful fisherman gave us a bucket of fresh-caught whelks, which we boiled immediately and ate that evening for tea (the only way whelks should be eaten, bearing no relation to those blobs of rubber preserved in vinegar): freights of cement, sand, more wheat. . . . Tides and winds and freight rates governed our daily lives in this strange new world.

The *Clara* was 82 feet long, and 19 feet wide; when deep loaded she needed some six feet three inches of water, when empty she could creep into even shallower water. She carried a maximum of five sails: there was no auxiliary power. To gather up the enormous mainsail when stowing it tight against the mast a powerful winch was used. This I could manage by myself. I could set the foresail, little mizzen, and tall light-weather staysail without help, but I did need an extra hand to set up the head of the great topsail. On each side of the ship hung the big wooden leeboards; these mysterious contrivances were lowered and hove up again on chains led aft to the crab winches. This also I could do unaided when required. There was a pair of davits set against the starboard quarter rail on which we hung our small boat when under way: only on short passages in the river did we leave the boat in the water and tow it astern. The steering compass reposed on a portable wooden pillar which could be bolted to the deck where it was readily visible to the steersman.

The cargo hold had two hatchways, the principal one abaft the mainmast, and a smaller one forward. Below decks the space between the main hold bulkhead and the stern post contained the crew's cabin, sometimes referred to by my skipper as the saloon. This we reached through a companionway with a sliding top and slots for two flashing boards to keep the water on deck from washing down into the cabin. The companionway could be locked on the outside with a padlock;

there was no way of securing it from the inside. A heavy wooden ladder slanted down into the cabin. Facing forward, there was a small cubbyhole which contained the calor gas stove and shelves for pots and pans. The cylinder of gas, contrary to regulations I'm afraid, stood on the floor beneath the stove. (There was, however, a strict rule, always complied with, that the bottle was to be turned off at the valve whenever the stove was not in use.) At this time all the other sailing barges' crews cooked on primus stoves and their cabin coal ranges which had a small oven. I was very lucky to have the gas cooker because I never could get the hang of a primus.

Against the forward bulkhead was the coal range which heated the cabin, dried a succession of wet clothes and kept the kettle singing on the hob. Facing aft, the view was of a tall narrow closet on the starboard side for storing clothes and seaboots; an enclosed bunk, built into each side of the cabin above cushioned lockers in which coal and firewood was stored, and a small hinged table. Abaft each bunk were panelled cupboards for food, crockery, etc. The thwartships cupboard right aft was called the Yarmouth Roads, because that's where we kept stocks of tinned food for use when lying windbound or fogbound for any length of time (as so often vessels lay weatherbound in the shelter of Yarmouth Roads when on the longer passages northward).

There was a large glass skylight let into the deck overhead, and when I first went aboard the artificial lighting was a large oil lamp which hung over the table. Later we progressed to a Tilley pressure lamp which, while still burning paraffin, gave a much brighter and harsher light with its incandescent mantle.

So, this small space was where the crew of a sailing barge spent their time on board when not working the ship. Here they slept, cooked, ate, washed, laundered, read books, played cards, listened to the radio, knitted jerseys, swapped yarns; when there were visitors, six people could just about be seated in a companionable huddle. There was no lavatory on board. The method of relief was to draw half a bucket of water from over the side and retire with it to the fo'c'sle, afterwards returning all to the sea. The fo'c'sle was quite roomy. There was a wooden bunk fitted to the port side, but usually it contained the various navigating lanterns, spare lamp chimneys, and a pile of old newspapers useful for cleaning and polishing the glasses. The rest of the fo'c'sle was a jumble of paint tins and brushes, spare rope, bundles of old scrap rope, tools, and a large coil of stayfall wire which was stowed down there when not needed for lowering the mast. Built into the fo'c'sle compartment was the chain locker where the barge's anchor cable was stored.

The *Clara* would usually carry whatever cargo was offered — to and from any of the small ports in Essex, Kent and Suffolk — between Ipswich in the north and Whitstable in the south. When not loading, carrying, and discharging cargo, we were kept busy with maintenance work on hull, sails and cordage. The skipper himself undertook all the minor work about the barge, when necessary with my ham-handed help. When the sails needed a patch or there was a tear to be darned, he would sit for hours with palm and needle, stitching away, herring-bone style. All I could do was keep the needles threaded; the sail-making palm he used was much too big for my hand. I did learn to do a bit of rope splicing; our ropes were usually old and worn and constant breaks had to be made good. I was never able to tackle wire-splicing, though the skipper was a dab hand at it.

All this took place in the last years before sailing barges were withdrawn from cargo carrying or converted to full power with most of their sails discarded (often retaining only a cut-down mast and a mainsail). I believe the stevedores used to hate to see us approaching. Compared with the simplicity of a modern motor barge we were indeed an awkward customer with our towering mast and sprit between the two holds, and forehatchway inconveniently small; our great clutter of sails and ropes to be kept clear, and the fact of our having no engine obliging every movement of the craft to be made by the crew pushing and pulling by hand. As soon as the dockers saw me aboard they would yell: "Got the kettle on, sailor?" We would bribe them with constant supplies of tea in the hope that they would put their best efforts into loading us as carefully and as quickly as they could. It would afford them great amusement to see me, with the skipper, wielding a sack hook, improving the stow in the 'wings' of the hold, or on top of a stack of timber with a timber hook nonchalantly heaving baulks of timber, three inches thick and twenty feet long, into the required position.

Having loaded, our usual method of getting the barge to the lock gate was to run a wire from the forward dolly winch as far along the dockside as we had length of wire, making the end fast on a bollard, then hauling it in, catching a turn on the quayside, running out the wire again, and again and *again* until we reached the end of the dock. Sometimes though, there would be a fair wind down to the gate, and if the dock wasn't obstructed by loose lighters we could sail down under topsail sheet only; or perhaps a friendly motor barge would give us a tow. Once out of the lock into the Thames there we were, depending entirely on the wind. If the wind happened to be between west and southwest and of moderate strength, we could just about make our way down the river without causing too much consternation amongst the other traffic. If there was any east in the weather, however, causing us to tack from side to side on very short boards, we must have been the object of much swearing from masters of big ships and tug skippers hauling strings of lighters — because strictly speaking vessels under power were supposed to give way to a vessel under sail alone (though in effect within such narrow waters there just wasn't enough room for ships to make drastic changes in course).

But our worst fate as far as I was concerned, was when there was no wind at all. The skipper was always loath to lose the opportunity of making some progress, and if the tide was on the ebb, and there was no wind, we used to just *drift* down the river, until we saw ourselves in danger of hitting some stationary object such as a quay or a tier of moored lighters. Then I would drop the anchor, so that it just touched the bottom, causing the *Clara* to sheer off in one direction or the other, according to the position of the rudder. At the crucial moment, the skipper would yell: *"Up anchor!"* whereupon I would have to wind frantically on the windlass handle until the 4 cwt anchor was clear of the river bed. Then we would continue with our drifting downstream, having neatly sidestepped the obstacle to our passage. This method of progression called for exact judgment on the skipper's part; all I needed to contribute was musclepower. So might I occupy the long hours of ebb: drop the anchor, haul it up (puff, puff, puff); drop the bloody thing again, haul it up — maybe twenty times over. How I used to *hate* a calm! Liberation from this treadmill was only granted when the tide turned and we were forced to anchor in earnest, or if lucky, tie up to a buoy or a tier of lighters, hoping a tug wouldn't come along to take the lighters away during our six hours spell of rest. I often thought any sailing barge under way without wind ought to be advertised in the Notices to Mariners as a "Navigational Hazard (intermittent)".

Once down below Gravesend in windless conditions it was often impossible to make progress by such means; the water was too deep. But once clear of the land it was unusual to be without any breath of air, and the spritsail barge is such an efficient design that any zephyr was enough to provide her with steerage way. The topsail was some 75 feet above the surface of the water and the light-weight staysail could be set above the heavy foresail; between them they could, most of the time, catch some small air of wind. Quite often when making our slow progress down Swin in such circumstances the sympathetic skipper of a motor barge, if he had a little time in hand, might fall alongside and take our ropes, so that we could make a joint progress down Swin — with the *Clara* travelling a whole lot faster, and the motor barge at only a little less than her usual speed.

Few sailing barges in my day had the luxury of a wheelhouse. The steersman must constantly leave the wheel to make adjustments to the sails, or peer round the bellying mainsail to see ahead, so that any kind of steering shelter was impracticable, and the crew was thus always exposed to the rain and the cold and the seaspray. One night in mid-winter when the *Clara* was bound to the Medway with a light northerly breeze astern, we had come up Swin in very dark and frosty conditions, and were carrying the last three hours of flood from the Blacktail Spit across to the Medway. There was not a lot of traffic in the Estuary that night and the barge required little more from her crew than a steady hand on the wheel. The skipper and I were bundled up in jerseys, duffels, woolly hats, scarves, gloves *and* mittens; twenty minutes was a as long as the steersman could tolerate before needing a warm up. Down below the fire was kept blazing and the cabin deliciously warm. How close I huddled to that fire — my feet practically on the bars and my gaze dreamily on the flames, absorbing the heat, and becoming very sleepy — until a guilty glance at the brass clock showed that it was time to go back on deck and take the place of my frozen skipper.

But it was not always winter in the Swin — nor always night; and that passage in a fine warm spell of moderate summer winds could compare with the happiest hours a wealthy yachtsman spends — anywhere in the world. Sometimes I think I felt just the smallest twinge of conscience when I thought of those at work ashore in offices and factories, while I could revel in clear blue skies and dancing waves and air that tasted like wine — and the certainty that I was going to be paid lovely money when the passage was over!

Chapter Two

The *Clara*'s World

WORKING in a sailing barge without the benefit of auxiliary power must surely have been one of the most exasperating ways anyone ever earned a living. Except on those rare occasions when the wind was fair and the seas moderate, it was a continual struggle to overcome any of a hundred adversities. Two centuries of development had produced a vessel capable of carrying between 100 and 200 tons of cargo, worked by a man and a boy, needing not much more than a fathom of water. That much said, however, it cannot be denied that they were ponderous brutes to operate. A great heavy pitchpine main mast, over forty feet tall, surmounted by a lesser spar of the same length which could be lowered down beside the main mast; an enormous sprit set at an angle from a point about five feet above the deck, never much less than sixty feet long, to hold the peak of the mainsail aloft and carry the sheet of the topsail — these and the heavy flax canvas attached to them were held aloft by a massive wire forestay and a six part tackle — of which more later. The sheet of the mainsail was controlled by five parts of rope and a massive block which hooked into an iron ring travelling from side to side of the after deck along a wooden beam (called a horse). The outer end of the sprit was held under control from the deck by means of two vangs terminating in four-part rope tackles. There was also in the *Clara* a small mizzen mast and sail aft which followed roughly the economy, though on a tiny scale, of her main gear. This was situated just abaft the steering wheel; in some of the big coasters the mizzen was very much larger and stepped forward of the steering wheel. That kind of barge also sported a bowsprit (as the *Clara,* by my day, did not — I always regarded a bowsprit barge as *very* superior).

Up forward, in the eyes of the ship, was the anchor windlass already referred to. Its wooden barrel carried three turns of cable, and relied wholly on the friction of two kinds of wood (the whelps), one hard, one soft, to restrain the chain from slipping out involuntarily. Our anchor

8

weighed 4 cwts. To hold a loaded barge in the London River with her gear aloft on a gale of wind and ebb tide, never less than fifteen fathoms of anchor chain was needed, often double that amount. Needless to say the gearing of the windlass was immensely powerful, for often a pull of several tons had to be overcome by the winding of a single person. Above the windlass was a smaller winch called a dolly which carried a long, fine, flexible wire, useful for extending many yards along the shore to enable a weary crew to heave the barge along without the benefit of the sails being set. The dolly winch was not geared in any way, but the precisely calculated diameter of the barrel and the powerful leverage of its two cranks were usually enough to enable the skipper and the mate between them to haul 200 tons or more of dead weight through the water.

The *Clara*'s sails with the single exception of the staysail (sometimes inaccurately called the flying jib) were coloured that evocative red-brown which came of a mixture of red and yellow ochre and fish oil — a preservative with which the sails were dressed annually by the crew. At the old shipyards on the south-east coast and other places where barges lay when not at work, there were areas of grass where the sails could be spread out for re-dressing. It was a job that ideally needed several hot, fine days. To begin with my skipper would go over the area picking out any stones or gravel which might be there, so as to avoid the possibility of treading them into and damaging the canvas. Then he'd mix the ochre and the fish oil in a drum and add several buckets of salt water. A great deal of mixing and stirring was needed before the right consistency was obtained. The fluid was next transferred into small containers and applied to the sails with long handled stiff bristled brushes, the crew taking great care to rub it well into the seams. If the sun was beating down, the skipper would have his shirt off, and we'd toil all day with only a short break for lunch, anxious that the job should be completed before dark, in case of a heavy dew in the night. Then it was necessary to leave them lying there on the grass perhaps for a couple of days to get thoroughly dry before once again being bent to the spars. Dressing sails is quite a pleasant job really — unless you object to the smell of fish oil!

Also attached to a sailing barge's hull are two of those fin-like iron bound wooden boards which so intrigue the passing landlubber. They are set either side amidships and act the same way as a keel — that is reducing the vessel's leeway when close-hauled. Being extremely heavy, they are lowered and raised by means of winches on the quarterdeck, the one in use being that on the opposite side to the wind: if the wind is on the starboard bow, then the port side leeboard is lowered — and vice versa. Once, berthed at Maldon I chalked this legend on the *Clara*'s shore-side leeboard: "It is to stop the barge going sideways. (And to stop you asking silly questions!)"

Barges, of course, were by their very nature required to go to wharves where deeper draught ships could not get, so most of our freights were taken to the very top end of the narrowest, twistiest, shallowest threads of creeks to be imagined. And of course, these places, being far inland would be crossed by at least one road bridge, fixed and immovable and very low-arched. So, if, for example, we were loaded with wheat for Marriage's mill at Colchester, we could only reach the North Quay under sail, and there we had to tie up and lower all the masts and sails — down nearly flush with the deck. What a performance! First the topmast was lowered to rest in front of the mainmast; then the anchor chain was taken from the barrel of the windlass and the stayfall brought up through a navel pipe from where it lay below the deck nestling against the chain locker. This wire was wound four times round the barrel of the windlass, vice the anchor chain, to be eased out very slowly indeed, allowing the masts and sprit to subside to the deck. Every few feet, the descent was halted while the skipper checked that all the running gear was free and not fouling something which might break or impede the lowering. Towards the end of this dangerous operation someone would have to stand under the end of the descending mast, holding a piece of stout timber, to shove under it at the very crucially correct moment, and at an equally critical angle so that everything might come to rest squarely. The mizzen mast was also lowered flat.

When the barge was due to lower her gear to go under a bridge it was usual for an assortment of people — crews of other barges lying nearby, old retired bargemen, eager youngsters — to muster on board. When there were half a dozen extra hands to keep an eye open all would go smoothly. We might also find a couple of men who were prepared to help us get through the bridges and the rest of the way up to East Mills. But when the last of the flood tide which we needed came at four in the morning this valuable aid was more usually lacking and it would be just the two of us. The only method of getting to the mill from below the bridges was to use setting booms — slender, 20-feet long poles, with which we shoved against the river bed up forward on either bow, walking along the deck until there was no more deck.

The boom then had to be dragged out of the soft mud and back we'd trot to the foredeck and repeat the process, again and again, until, hopefully by high water the mill was reached. And having got there after all that poking and shoving, nothing could be done about the cargo until all those masts and sails had been hauled into an upright position again. Often there were other barges with us in the pool outside the mill, the crews gave one another a hand with the raising of the gear. It was hove up, of course, on the anchor windlass, with many pauses for breath and to check that all the ropes and wires were clear. Four strong bargemen were none too many for that labour.

After taking off the hatchcloth and the hatches, there we were — all ready for unloading. When that was completed the whole performance must needs be repeated in reverse: On hatches, down mast, poke with the poles backwards down the creek; and while there had to be enough water to float us under the bridge, there mustn't be too much, or we would swim too high to get under! Many's the barge that made a gleeful photo in the local press having been caught trying to get under on the flood — only to be squashed beneath the arch by the rising tide! We never did that, but we did on one occasion get beneaped under the bridge at East Mills trying to get up to unload on a poor tide, and remained there for several days until a new lot of springs came round. It's very dark, living under a bridge: we had to keep the cabin lamp alight all day long!

*   *   *

Trading with a sailing barge in winter time could certainly be a miserable business. Day after day, tacking from one side of the buoyed channel to the other, making a few miles progress with each tide; often spending all day working on deck soaked to the skin and frozen with cold (though, oddly enough, very rarely catching a cold); hauling on ropes saturated with salt water, which caused painful fissures at the ends of fingers; struggling with stiff, heavy, wet canvas, and handling ice-cold winch handles.

At the end of a long, tiring voyage, when the anchor was in the ground, came the necessary business of tidying up the ship; stowing the topsail aloft, brailing in the mainsail as tightly as possible, giving a loose stow to the foresail, getting the riding light up from the fo'c'sle if it was growing dark — this and many more minor tasks needed to be done before the passage could be considered complete. Now, in other barges that I knew, all this work was shared by the skipper and the mate before they retired to the cabin, where the skipper could put his feet up and smoke a cigarette and generally take his ease, while the mate bustled about getting a meal cooked — and afterwards clearing it away. Only when he'd done the washing up could the poor, wretched mate subside on to his own locker and relax for the rest of the evening.

As mate of the *Clara,* I was much better used. After we'd come to anchor, the skipper and I would set about the aforementioned tasks around the decks, but at a certain point (and it was always timed very nicely) the skipper would say to me: "Right-o, I'll finish off up here; you go and get the dinner." What a relief! Down I'd go into the welcome warmth of the cabin — and aim to have the meal ready on the table when the skipper came down the cabin ladder. How grateful I was for this thoughtful and eminently sensible division of labour.

"There are old skippers and there are bold skippers, but there are *no* bold, old skippers . . ." That is the maxim my captain taught to me. We sometimes had to lie at anchor under Shotley Spit in the Ipswich river, in company with perhaps half a dozen sailormen bound for London; some loaded, some light with orders to load, and the *Clara* most often light and bound only for Woolwich buoys (where if luck came her way she would receive some orders). We might be riding out a south-westerly gale and when it fined away to only half a gale, and backed southerly, and the sun was shining, a couple of bold cases might get under way and stretch out across Dovercourt Bay with the prospect of a long turn to windward, up the Wallet and the Swin. Often, when I was all impatient to follow them out to sea instead of enduring another tedious unproductive day swinging around the anchor off H.M.S. *Ganges,* my skipper would shake his head and quote the recent unfavourable forecast, stating solemnly (putting it on a bit): "You mark my words, that wind will veer round again soon and freshen, and we'd only end up back here, *if* nothing worse!" Sometimes his decision was vindicated — especially if the intrepid ones came back in again, some hours later, with all their gear saturated, decks and hatchways washed *very* clean, and maybe a split in the topsail to be mended. On such occasions he would say: "Well, that's saved them from having to scrub round the decks!"

On the other hand, the weather could give him a poke in the eye and we'd waste a perfectly reasonable flood tide which might have carried us up through the Spitway by high water to an anchorage under Foulness when the ebb started down. These lost opportunities never seemed to make him morose; his personal philosophy was that it was better to lose a tide than gain a passage at the expense of a hundred pounds worth of damage to the gear.

Looking at an ordinary land map of the area that stretches from the North Foreland, near Margate, taking in the north coast of Kent, the Thames Estuary and the Essex and Suffolk coasts, it would seem that a ship might sail down the Thames, and, if bound for Brightlingsea for instance, just continue along the coast, round Shoeburyness, Foulness Island, and make a bee-line northwards to the entrance of the River Colne. Unfortunately, this can only be done (at some considerable peril) by a very shallow draught vessel on the very top of the high water. One of the dangers is that at ebb tide a wide area of the Maplin Sand quickly comes a-dry; another is that several miles of the coast from Shoeburyness to the River Crouch belong to the Ministry of Defence, and the sands are used as an artillery range. England is (allegedly) a free country and the War Department does not try to stop vessels from sailing over the firing range; but due warning is given on the chart and by the flying of red flags and I believe anyone being accidentally hit by shot or shell would not have much of a legal leg to stand on.

So out there beyond the Maplin Sand is the first of the shipping channels, the West Swin, much used by barges and small coasters bound north. The Swin is generously marked with conical and can buoys on either side, some with flashing lights, some "blind". There are also two or three old wooden beacons with various topmarks to help sailors identify their position, and in the fifties there was a wrecked ship on the Barrow Sand, whose tangled masts were an excellent seamark in daytime. The Barrow Sand is the seaward boundary of the Swin and beyond it is a channel known as the Barrow Deep, used by the big ships and most of the larger coasters from foreign and home waters. The Barrow Deep in my day boasted its own light vessel which I never saw but whose voice in thick weather was our constant companion — a completely unmistakable voice which I can only describe as *burrrr-ump!*

So with the Essex coast guarded by many square miles of sands, our vessel sailed almost beyond the sight of land down the West Swin. The first low way was at the end of the Buxey Sand, to the south-east of Clacton, which led into the Wallet. This very narrow gap between the Buxey and the Gunfleet Sands was called the Spitway and was thought so important to inshore seamen that Trinity House provided it with a light buoy at the southern end and a large red and white striped bell-buoy at the northern end. Nowadays, not only has the Spitway been moved a couple of miles nearer to the Essex shore because of a shift in the sands, (a boon to those working into the Colne) but also has *both* ends lit. Such luxury!

So, that area of seemingly innocent, smooth, uninterrupted sea, bounded about by Clacton, Margate and Southend becomes, at half ebb, a system of banks often covered by only inches of water, and at low tide a maze of sandhills and deep valleys, the whole thing in an unpredictable state of movement at the whim of easterly weather.

*   *   *

One dark night the *Clara* was drifting down Swin in very light airs, and I was standing up forward keeping a lookout. Suddenly I became aware of the approach of — *what?* An unlit ship perhaps, or maybe a sea monster? From the merest rustling of the water, the noise slowly increased to a tremendous rushing and bubbling. Then I saw what it was. I made a quick calculation as to which way we were being set by the tide, and yelled to the skipper at the wheel: *"Hardaport!"* Fortunately the barge had steerage way to answer her helm. We sheered off to port. The great, lumping Maplin buoy, unlit, rushed along our starboard side and was soon out of sight. Of course the buoy itself was securely moored to the sea bed; it was *us* being carried down the Swin by a fast tide, despite there being so little wind. This kind of minor incident, by no means uncommon in the days of sail, which sometimes led to shipwreck, serves to illustrate those perils of the Thames Estuary which are unknown to deep water mariners. I suppose we sailormen must mostly have known the Swin in its more benign moods: moderate winds, calms and fogs; the bargemen did not wish to be out there in a gale of wind from any quarter, especially anything with an easterly slant about it. But of course there were occasions when we risked it for the sake of a temptingly fair wind for London or for Ipswich, or on what looked like a fine day whilst at anchor in the Colne, and later turned into a gale of wind from the south-east. It was not often that we were caught out by the weather; but when we were it was a case of pounding on, heeling over, leeboard flared out, loose rope ends flying out to leeward, on our beam ends, seas constantly washing right across the hatchways, the lee deck always a foot beneath the surface. All the loose gear on deck — mooring ropes, sweeps, ladders, hitchers, had to be lashed down on the hatches with miles of thin line; all eventually ended up in an unholy tangle in the lee scupper. Perhaps at last the skipper would say to the mate that they'd better take in some of the mainsail before it blew away, and the mate would choose the moment and nip along the lee deck, ducking under the foot of the taut and dripping mainsail, to find the winch handle and start winding in the main brail, a pawl or two at a time, ducking into the comparative shelter of the mastcase when a great cold sea flung itself, hissing and roaring, over the windward deck, then back to heave another inch or two of wire on the winch. The skipper would need to put the lock on the wheel while he slacked off the main sheet and pulled in the weather vang. Both he and the mate would, of course, be soaked to the skin. After many hours in this state, the fingers would turn white and wrinkled with the cold salt water, and cuffs would rub sore patches on wrists, so that every movement of the hands was torture. But sooner or later, perhaps after many hours of enduring frozen, aching muscles, eyes smarting with salt spray and the lesser pangs of hunger and thirst which often had to go unsatisfied in a ship manned by only two people, the voyage would end. Then with all the heavy labour of stowing the sails and bringing up accomplished, the warmth and comfort of the cabin was paradise. "Well, we got here!" Yes, we got here, and it wasn't so bad, really, was it? "We had a good old sail, didn't we? I don't reckon we wet more than a few hundred-weights of wheat . . ."

It was at moments like that a barge mate could feel genuinely sorry for those poor devils ashore. What sort of existence did they have? Never *really* wet; never *really* cold; never more than a little bit hungry — never properly alive. Who would want to change places with them? — not I! Not once the cabin fire was alight and the kettle boiling merrily on the trivet.

An hour later after, getting into dry clothing and outside a hot meal, I wouldn't want to change places even with the Queen of England! That's barging for you! That's the *real* magic.

Chapter Three

Red Sails in the City

THE *Clara* often found herself on the barge mooring at Woolwich. This is on the north side of the London river just below the Free Ferry and has been, for many generations, the place where sailing barges come to await their orders for the next freight. Such was the polluted state of the river thirty years ago that if we lingered there for more than a couple of days all the brasswork on deck and in the cabin would be turned blue by the gases given off by the water.

During the hungry thirties the Woolwich mooring was known as the starvation buoys and dozens of barges out of work lay there, a veritable forest of masts, swinging to every tide for weeks on end. In the nineteen-fifties the *Clara* occasionally lay at Woolwich in company with another half dozen craft, but within a couple of days of arrival each skipper got his orders to go and load somewhere and would slip away, to be replaced by a new arrival, usually sailed up light from Essex or Kent. There was a continual coming and going at Woolwich buoys. If we thought, hopefully, that we might be there for only a few hours, we wouldn't trouble to put our own rope on the buoy but would tie up to the outer barge of the tier. Otherwise, when we came up alongside, we'd first catch a turn on one of the others, then there was sure to be a mate who'd jump into his boat, take the end of our rope over the bow and make a long bowline in the ring on the buoy. Then skippers and mates from the other barges would come swarming aboard. The skippers would congregate aft to find out where we'd come from, and if we'd got any orders, where we were going to, generally gleaning all the latest gossip. The mates would help me tidy up the barge: heave down hard on the topsail clewline so that the loose ends wouldn't flap in the wind, stow the foresail into a narrow tidy parcel and heave it up the forestay out of the way, and brail in the mainsail and haul tight on the middles and lowers. So the tidying up which would have taken me half an hour was all got through in five minutes with the help of willing hands, and then we could relax. Some

(1) *Clara* photographed when new.

(2) Some of my predecessors working on the *Clara*. My father told me that bargemen were lower than street-sweepers; that I wouldn't stick the job for more than six weeks. I stuck it for fourteen years.

(4) Calm at eventide. The life was hard, but at moments like this I would not
have changed places with the Queen of England. I sailed with the same
skipper for fourteen years; so often his great sense of humour kept us from
despair.

Left: (3) The *Clara* wending. Foresail held 'aback' on the bowline presses the barge's
head round on to the new tack.

Above left: (5)   The timber wharf at Maldon, where I first saw the *Clara*.

Below left: (6)   This auxiliary barge, bound up to Maldon, shows the method of loading a deck cargo of timber.

Above: (7)   At the other end: a tier of barges wait on a mooring buoy.

Above: (8) 'Grab' work — unkind to hatchway coamings. Note the stack of hatches aft: these will be replaced when discharging is complete — or hastily during unloading if it begins to rain.

Right, top: (9) A Colchester-owned barge with gear lowered flat. The crew would always be glad of some extra help on the windlass handles to heave up the heavy spars and sails from this vast angle. All too often, however, the two of us would have to struggle on our own.

Below: (10) At Marriage's mill, Colchester. Sailing barge lowering down gear ready to go away through bridges. The *Leofleda*'s crew have gone aboard to help.

(11)   Loaded barges sail away out of Colne.

time later the skipper and I would scull ashore in our boat. He'd go to the phone to announce our arrival to our agents, the London and Rochester Trading Company, and I'd repair to the nearest shops to replenish our supply of groceries, and, of course, to buy an evening paper.

And so the humdrum pattern of the *Clara*'s voyagings would continue. In those final years of the last few trading spritsail barges they slogged about the Thames Estuary and adjacent rivers for the most part without dramatic incident and very largely out of the limelight (a great contrast with those darlings of the tourists today, the expensively refurbished remnants of the fleet lying idly by, foreground scenery in St Katharine's Dock yacht marina). I would like to take the reader on with the *Clara* from Woolwich buoys to show a typical workaday sequence of ordinary passages achieved, and just what work was involved for a sailing barge crew to earn a crust. Uneventful? Yes and no . . .

On this day, for example, the skipper came back on board from the phone with no orders for the barge but with instructions to speak to the agents again next morning. After supper he went visiting with his cronies who were crowded into the cabin of one of the other barges, leaving me alone to settle down with a book and the radio, weary after a long day's work turning up the river against the wind, and I was asleep in my bunk before the skipper returned. The next morning he went ashore again and at ten o'clock he returned with orders to tow up river to Chelsea to load flour for Aylesford, round on the Medway. A tug had been ordered for us and was expected at about half flood; in the meantime we had to lower the mast ready for passing beneath the London bridges. It didn't have to be lowered flat, only about two-thirds (so the mast prop was much longer than the one used when we went up to the mill at Colchester). Willing hands helped with the lowering, and we had time to get our dinner in comfort before the tug appeared. The tug had three loaded lighters in tow, and we moored up alongside the third one, making it two pairs in tandem.

In that fashion we proceeded up river through the several bridges to the mill where we were to load. We had plenty of time to get the gear hove upright again as we were not due to take on our cargo until morning. Rain was pouring down all that afternoon and we had to leave the hold covered to keep it dry. In the morning at 7 o'clock it was still raining and when loading commenced we only uncovered sufficient of the hold to take the chute, in an attempt to keep the ceiling dry for the cargo. Sacks of flour slid down the wooden chute. Four stevedores worked in the hold, each one catching a descending sack on his shoulder, humping it under the wings, and depositing it in a cloud of flour dust on the floor of the hold until the stack under the side decks was shoulder high. Then they moved the operation inwards towards the centre of the hold until the whole area was covered. The chute was then retracted to a high level and the procedure repeated until the main cargo space was filled. We replaced the few hatches and drew the cloth over them, hauling the barge further along the wharf, to suit the chute, made a gap in the forehatchway, and loading once again proceeded in the same manner. Throughout the whole operation rain fell without relent.

When the men stopped for an hour at midday we went ashore and had our own lunch at a nearby café and I went to the shop to buy provisions for what we hoped would be a quick passage.

After loading was complete we finished covering up and battening down the hatches. Then we lowered down the masts again and were ready for the tug to tow us back down to the Lower Pool. They dropped us off on a tier of lighters just below Tower Bridge. Here once again we hove up the gear — but it was long after high water and coming dark, so the skipper decided to lie at Wapping overnight and make an early start in the morning to catch the tide. I had kept the fire burning all day so that the cabin was warm and snug. Soon our wet clothes hung gently steaming on lines strung under the deckhead around the stovepipe while our shoes dried out against the fender. (We didn't often wear wellington boots, the skipper reckoned they were bad for the feet.) I fried some sausages. By the time we'd cleared away the meal, listened to the weather forecast and done the crossword puzzle in the *Daily Express,* it was time to turn in.

At two o'clock next morning we were once again up and about; after a quick mug of tea I went to the fo'c'sle and lit the navigation lamps and brought them on deck, where the skipper hoisted them into place in the rigging. When I had fixed the stern lamp on its bracket we were ready to set the topsail and let go our moorings. It was pleasant enough, despite the rain, sailing an old barge down the London river in the dark. There is always less traffic in the night, and those who needed to be about had passed us an hour ago, intent on getting to their berths as soon as there was water. A moderate breeze about force 4 was blowing from the south-west. The *Clara* slipped silently through the dark water, dappled with silver from reflected street and wharf lights. Soon the skipper was asking for more sail. I dragged the main sheet block aft and hooked it into the ring on the main horse, then let go the middles and lowers and eased out part of the main brail until he shouted: "Right that'll do!" He left the wheel and hauled the sheet tight, slacking off the starboard vang to suit our sail to the wind. As soon as the *Clara* was clear below Woolwich she needed the rest of her mainsail; and we fairly sped downstream past sleeping wharves, factories and tank farms, and into the mouth of the river Medway. Here we anchored, close in among the marshes, opposite the Isle of Grain oil terminal. We had eaten a good breakfast while under way, so as soon as the sails were stowed up we were able to snatch a couple of hours' rest.

Now it was time to turn out again and make tacks up the Medway — and still raining as if it was never going to stop. On board the *Clara* the shortage of dry clothing was becoming acute. As we crossed, close-hauled, from bank to bank in the narrowing reaches of the Medway, my station was by the foresail, ready to let it go every time we came about on a word from the man at the wheel. Of shelter from that relentless driving rain there was none, save that offered by the lee of the sail. We arrived at Strood buoys near high water and moored alongside a motor barge. I boated the skipper ashore to the office where he learned we were booked to get a tow up the river with one of the local motor barges the following day.

The only bridge across the Medway below Aylesford at that time was the Rochester road and rail bridge, but it could not be opened for shipping to pass, so we had to lower the masts to get through. This we did after tea that evening, so that we should be all ready to tow up the river next day when the motor barge crew turned up. They arrived early in the afternoon.

We towed lashed alongside, and as soon as we were through the bridge two of the crew of the motor barge stepped across to help us heave our gear up once again — a heavy job for only two people; as I have said, bargemen always helped each other in this way. Past the Halling cement works, backed by the great cliffs left by the quarry works, then through meandering reaches, the river narrowing all the while, at last we reached Aylesford and just managed to pass under a gantry (our topmast had remained housed), to take a berth beneath the high roof of the mill. The rain had never left off since we loaded and had found the faults in our hatchcloth. When we started to uncover the main hatchway we saw that the tops of some of the sacks

had got wet, and this displeased the foreman who came to take charge
of our unloading.

The discharge took two full days, by which time we had our next
orders: to get down to Halling, just above Rochester Bridge, and load
cement there for a ship in Tilbury Dock. One of the Trading
Company's little tugs came to tow us down to the cement factory and
we got loaded without any of the usual delays.

Cement must be one of the dustiest freights there is (if you don't
count Turkish barley). Every surface of the enormous factory was
inches deep in the stuff, and all the surrounding vegetation was grey. It
clung to the roofs of the nearby houses, and windows and doors were
kept tight shut in an effort to control its infiltration. The factory
workers, too, were covered in dust, the same grey colour from the tops
of their cotton hats to the tips of their stout boots. So, too, were the
crews of the barges loading there. A great cloud, grey and clinging,
hung all about us. We shut the cabin and the fo'c'sle hatches in an
attempt to keep it out; nevertheless it found its way down below to
permeate everywhere. I discovered one curious thing about cement:
I've got dead straight hair, but with the addition of a generous dusting
of cement powder it became quite wavy; grey of course, but with a
definite curl to it.

Some of the bags split during the loading and we had to keep count
of them for they must be noted when signing the bill of lading,
otherwise the barge would be held responsible at the time of
discharging. We finished loading well before the next tide, got covered
up, lowered down the gear and towed down to Strood buoys. Once
through the bridge we moored temporarily — to raise once again those
heavy sails and spars.

Then we could sail away down river on the last of the ebb and with a
favourable slant of wind. Out in the broad estuary we began tacking
up Sea Reach (past Southend Pier) now helped by the incoming
Thames tide, to anchor finally in the Lower Hope a few miles below
Gravesend. There was plenty of time in hand for this freight; the ship
we were to discharge into was not expected until the following week, so
there were several designated laydays in our contract and no hope of
demurrage payment unless the ship's arrival was later than predicted.
We upped anchor early on the flood tide next day and were able to
lock into the Tilbury Dock before there was too much activity there.
Even so, we did have to hang on outside for an hour to wait for another
ship to go in, as they wouldn't usually open those big gates for only one

humble little sailing barge.

Tilbury Dock was in a quiet state at the time and using the trackline we hove our way unimpeded along the quays until we came to an out of the way wharf where several other barges were lying in wait for ships to arrive. The skipper went off home for the weekend. I pottered about the barge, filling oil lamps and cleaning their glasses and giving the cabin a much needed clean up. Then I did my laundry, accumulated over the past couple of weeks, and hung it out to dry on a line stretched between the boat davits. On Saturday I took the ferry over to Gravesend to look at the shops and on my way back filled two shopping bags with replenishments for the grub locker. Milk was usually a problem on board the *Clara*; neither skipper nor mate cared for the tinned milk which most crews used. Fresh milk wouldn't keep more than a day, but sterilised in bottles would keep indefinitely until the bottle was opened. It was not then widely sold so if I did come across it I would buy six bottles at a time, a heavy burden to carry any distance.

Victualling the ship in my day generally entailed a good healthy walk enjoying dockland scenery, shopping bags loaded to the gunwales. Nowadays they tell me about a prodigal use of taxis instead of feet; even of smart vans delivering provisions to the quayside, virtually straight into a ship's refrigerator. My goodness; down the Swin with a fridge . . . how extraordinarily luxurious!

*   *   *

The skipper came back aboard the following Tuesday. Our ship still hadn't shown up and we could get a little maintenance done about the barge; patching the worst places in the hatchcloth, cobbling up smaller tears with herringbone stitches. I kept the skipper supplied with threaded sail needles and went around working grease into his neat mends.

Our ship, one of the Union Castle line, arrived that night and early next morning several barges were clustered around her high pink sides. Her derricks were kept busy loading, from the quayside in the one direction and from our side in the other. However we had to wait our turn and were not started that day, though needed to remain close by in case we were called: we lay alongside the ship throughout the night and only started discharging after the dockers' morning tea break. It was necessary to swing our sprit as far away from the ship as it would go so as not to foul her gear. Then we uncovered the main hatchway. Six

dockers came down the ship's ladder and the derrick swung over us to
deposit on top of the sacks of cement a small wooden platform slung
from chains at its corners. A couple of dozen bags were lifted on to it;
the man standing at the ship's rail gave the signal to lift, which was
passed on to the invisible donkeyman who lifted and swung the load
out of sight and dropped it into the depths of the big ship's hold.

As soon as the dockers spotted me, there was the inevitable shout of:
"Got the kettle on Mister Mate?" I went down below and made a big
pot of tea, pouring it into a disparate array of mugs, and taking it up
on deck together with a bowl of sugar. (Sugar was still rationed, even
this long after the end of the war, but seamen got an extra ration —
perhaps to take account of the amount of tea we had to give to the
dockers when they were working aboard us!) They were always very
polite and thanked me. Also, they were much more careful with their
language then, than nowadays, when women seem to use the same
vulgar speech as men. I notice today that men no longer mince their
words in female company — a reflection of the unisex fashion. Thirty
years ago, although the dockers employed the usual monotonous
expletives among themselves, whenever I appeared on deck one was
sure to hiss: "Watch out, woman aboard!" and at once the vocabulary
became blameless, hardpressed though they must have been to find an
acceptable adjective!

Unloading the cement was slow. We didn't finish that day and had
to cover up the hold for the night for fear of rain, and uncover again
next morning, folding back the canvas sheets and lifting the heavy
wooden hatches. They finished the main hold before lunch next day
and moved on to the smaller forehold. Extra care with the derrick was
needed here to avoid becoming entangled with our forestay, but with
the aid of two more pots of tea, they finished discharging us by mid-
afternoon and we immediately shoved clear of the ship to let in the
lighter next to be unloaded. A motor barge, unloaded at the same time
as us was going out of the dock to lie on a mooring buoy at Grays. He
kindly offered to tow the *Clara*: this of course we gladly took advantage
of, and locked out of the Tilbury Dock alongside him. At Grays, in the
next bight of the river, we lay comfortably enough for the weekend;
there were no orders for us yet. Again the skipper went home.

I had just finished my tea and was listening to the radio and doing
some knitting when there was a commotion above. A couple of rings on
an engineroom telegraph, the sudden rush of a propeller going astern,
a gentle bump, and a small river tug was alongside the *Clara*. "You

here for the weekend, sailorman?" one of the crew inquired. I nodded. "Can you give us a shove ashore in about half an hour then?" I said I could. When the three members of the tug's crew were ready in their gabardine raincoats and trilby hats, the skipper carrying a small grip, they stepped into our small boat and I sculled them over to the hard, holding the boat against the concrete while they stepped ashore. They thanked me and strode up the causeway into the town. As I pushed off from the hard, I was amazed and delighted to see a half crown piece on the thwart! I had not expected a tip, though the skipper told me afterwards that it was the usual practice. But Moses! Half a crown! I shall never forget the thrill of money so casually earned!

The skipper came back on Monday with the remains of a Sunday joint, a loaf of fresh bread, and the morning paper. He had phoned the London office and we were wanted up in the KGV as quickly as we could get there — to load cheese!

We got under way at once and made a fairly fast passage up the Thames with the wind fresh and southerly. A few long tacks in some of the upper reaches and we arrived outside the King George V Dock entrance. After locking in, we worked our way laboriously up to the far end of the dock having to wait for a man to open a couple of footbridges spanning the narrow cut which joined the two sections of this great dock.

The *Clara* was able to sail the greater part of the distance, but at the far end, where the ship we wanted was lying, the way was choked with dozens of drifting lighters and it was pull and push, heave and sweat to force a passage through them. Sometimes one of us would hop from lighter to lighter, some distance ahead to look for the easiest route (like down in the Antarctic where a helicopter leaves the mother ship to seek out the best lead through the icepack!) "I think if we pull round the stern of *this* one, then shove that one away to port, we can haul ourselves along the length of that one, with the blue hatchcloth. Then we'll have a clear space as far as the one loaded with timber . . ." etc. Most of the pushing was done with our feet, backs first against the bow rail, then against the rigging and finally against the quarterboards and the boat davits. A last mighty shove, and leap back aboard, hoping that the impetus given to the lighter would carry it clear of our rudder, though it could so often happen that a puff of wind would give the offending lighter a sheer back in our direction, and it would try to snuggle in alongside us. All very frustrating. On some occasions it might take hours to move a few hundred yards in a crowded dock. But eventually, on this day, we soon saw the name of the ship we were seeking, and could moor up gratefully to one of the lighters clustered around her sides. The skipper went up the ship's ladder and returned shortly with the news that they wanted us on the inside, between the ship and the dockside. This was always awkward for us, having a tall mast to pass under the ship's mooring ropes. (The ship was held clear of the dockside by great wooden pontoons.) After half an hour of toil at last we arranged the *Clara* under the derrick that worked the ship's forehold. We had already uncovered our own hold; the moment we hauled the sprit out of the way the first load of cheese was swung aboard.

The cheeses were packed, in pairs, into cylindrical slatted wooden cases (perhaps so they could breathe?) and the cases came aboard several at a time in a rope net hung from the derrick's hook, to be gently deposited in our hold where the stevedores rolled them first into the wings under the sidedecks and into the cupboard aft, working all the time towards the kelson. It was a slow process and it took several hours to fill the main hold. We went ashore for lunch at one of the dockers' canteens. Later, back on board with the loading again in progress, I was down in the cabin when the skipper called to me to come on deck. Quietly he said to me "Look what the men are doing in the hold. Don't say anything." I leaned casually against the coaming and glanced into the hold. Two of the stevedores were under the mastcase where they couldn't be seen from the decks of the ship and were painstakingly at work on one of the crates with a long sharp knife inserted between the wooden slats. By making one long cut, then shaking the cheese round a couple of inches and making another cut, a large wedge shaped slice of cheese could be slid out through the gap between the slats. The cheese was then moved around inside the case again and another cut made, producing yet another wedge. The skipper went down into the hold and shortly afterwards returned with a mysterious bulge under his jacket which he transferred to our store cupboard in the cabin. He had brought two pieces of cheese which must have weighed a couple of pounds each — of most delicious New Zealand cheddar. The two men down in the hold laboured on industriously at their disgraceful task until each man had a supply hidden on his person. With the operation complete the raped case of cheese was stowed away out of sight, in the darkest part of the hold.

We ate cheese sandwiches, had cheese sauce on our sausages, cheese on our toast — cheese with everything for two weeks after. A welcome

treat for a hungry crew after those long years of wartime rationing
when a week's cheese ration was only a couple of ounces per person.
Which reminds me of the time we loaded a freight of split peas, and I
filled all our spare utensils with the spillage of the hold, and for a
month had dinners of pea soup flavoured with knuckle ends of ham,
eventually getting the feeling that split peas were growing out of our
ears! I've never much cared for the dish since then. . . .

Well, eventually we finished loading our precious and aromatic
cargo, covered the hatches and worked our way wearily back down the
length of the dock to the lock gates. We tucked the *Clara* into the lock
in front of an enormous freighter, to be shortly ejected into the
tideway. It was just about high water and there was a lot of jostling
outside the lock with two ships and their attendant tugs manoeuvring
in the middle of the river. Rather than add to the confusion we slid
round the corner of the lock and caught a turn on the wooden piles to
wait for the traffic to disperse. There was just the one rope out forward
and I was still making it fast when I heard a shout from the skipper aft
at the wheel. Looking up, I saw that the ship which had followed us
out of the lock was headed fast out into the middle of the river and
seemed in imminent danger of colliding with the bow of an equally
large ship standing off the lock entrance. Again I heard the skipper
shout, but the sound was mixed up with frantic hoots from tugs and
other ships and I thought: "Hammer!" was what he shouted. I couldn't
understand what he would want with a hammer, but mine not to
reason why; he was jumping up and down and it sounded urgent, so I
quickly searched around until I found the big wedge hammer and
handed it to him. He flung it from him in a fury and shouted:
"Camera! Camera!" I leaped down into the cabin and brought up my
little camera but of course by that time the best of it was over. The two
ships had collided bow on and were now sliding apart, leaving one with
a slightly twisted stem and the other with a dented bow plate and a
broken rail. The skipper was very cross, muttering: "Could have been
worth hundreds, a good photo of that," and I flared up: "Well, I
thought you wanted a hammer!" "Bah!" was all I got, and it was at
least five minutes before he could bring himself to speak to me again.
One thing about the skipper, he never held a grudge for long, despite
the many occasions I must have caused him serious annoyance with my
ham-handed incompetence. I, on the other hand, was never able to
sulk because he just refused to notice, and it needs two for a quarrel.
Perhaps he balanced my stupidity and ineptitude against a moderate

cooking ability, and (being impervious to weather) my rarely being sick at sea.

After that excitement, and with the river comparatively clear of traffic we set the topsail and pushed out into the fairway and off down as far as the Hope anchorage where we rounded to on the last of the ebb and caught a turn on a vacant mooring buoy.

These buoys are intended for large ships — they are great floating iron cylinders with an iron ring on top. They are ribbed with pieces of timber which provide a useful foot grip for anyone like me who has to clamber over them with the end of a rope in one hand. The skipper would decide which way the tide was setting on to the buoy and bring the barge up alongside it so that the tide pinned her to it. I would be ready with the end of a good rope to leap from the deck to buoy, pass the end through the ring and jump back aboard with it before the buoy soaked away from the barge, then make fast both ends of the rope after paying out sufficient for us to lie comfortably clear. Thus when we came to let go all I had to do was to cast off the short end and we would drift clear. On one memorable occasion, whilst performing this manoeuvre, I wasn't quick enough in getting the end through the ring before the buoy slipped clear of the barge and began to surge from side to side in the grip of the tide. There was I left clinging on for dear life. The skipper had to sheer the barge into shallow water, let go the anchor and come and rescue me in the boat. Most embarrassing to be left sitting there somewhat after the fashion of the little mermaid at Kobenhavn.

There was an occasion even more humiliating when some years later we were to bring the *Dingle* up to Rainham, below Gillingham on the Medway. We arrived at the entrance to the creek before there was sufficient water for us, and the skipper proposed to catch a turn on a mooring buoy there to save dropping the anchor. This was somewhat smaller than the big ship buoys, and spherical in shape. We had a youth aboard as a temporary third hand. Coming alongside the buoy I stepped on to it, holding on with one hand and with the other outstretched to take the end of the rope from the youth. But the buoy refused to maintain its equilibrium under my weight and slowly rotated, finally tipping me gently into the water. I feel it was much to the credit of the third hand and the skipper that they managed to keep the grins off their faces as they hauled me back aboard.

But to dispose of that cheese . . . We lay the flood in the Hope and the next ebb drifted down Sea Reach and tied up on a tier of lighters outside Queenborough. Next day we towed alongside a motor barge through Kingsferry Bridge (no need to lower the masts for that one!). Then into narrow Milton Creek to Sittingbourne where we discharged our very slightly mutilated freight of cheese into a warehouse.

Our next orders were to load paper out of a ship lying off Rochester, for discharge at Thames Board Mills at Purfleet. So we worked up the Medway again, to find a large Swedish ship already unloading on both sides of all holds, barges and lighters swarming all around. Then it was our turn to load, and for this freight a tally was required, so I sat on the main horse with a notebook and pencil and counted the bundles as they swung aboard. They were in special slings designed to avoid damaging the expensive and vulnerable paper; the number of bundles in each sling varied, so I had to be careful with my tally as it was required to agree with that of the tallyman on the ship's deck. My tallies *never* came out exact, but within reasonable limits nobody seemed to worry. Sometimes the tallyman on the ship, who I believe was keeping count out of more than one hold at the same time, would lean out over the rail of the ship and shout to me: "How many in that last sling, sailor?" He'd missed it as it swung over us. As the bales were very big we were soon full up in the hold and the skipper went on loading until he had a fair sized stack of bales on deck which we only just managed to cover using every hatchcloth we had. With a stack on board, we needed to tie up the foot of the mainsail so that it could pass clear over the deck cargo. We had a fair wind down the Medway, but soon we came out into Sea Reach where it was once again to be tack and tack every inch of the way up the Thames. Having repeatedly to clamber over the stack only added to this wearisome work. The skipper stood up on a box at the wheel when he wanted to see ahead. When the tide was done we had to bring up. And again, and again. Three high waters passed us before we arrived at Purfleet.

Because they were not ready to unload us we lay here a further day and a night before lowering the topmast and going under the gantry. Paper mills are permeated with the most revolting smell and there was a visible population of rats on the stacks of pulp stored around the wharf. Two days there was two days too long, and we were glad to get away and sail on up the river to the buoy at Woolwich. We lay a weekend and got orders on the Monday to load wheat in the Victoria Dock for Felixstowe. This cheered us up because it would be a better paid freight than those we carried between the Thames and the Medway. Remember, there was no regular weekly wage, so the financial

＊ WOODPULP

aspect of our orders was always of vital interest to us. (That cheese freight, by the way, was termed a "minimum freight", because it was extremely light weight relative to its bulk, and mere tonnage would have left the payment for the freight below the minimum.)

One of the motor barges on the buoy was also bound for the Victoria Dock and kindly offered to give us a tow up the reach, through the lock and up to the grain silo; with that we were well content.

We loaded that afternoon. The dusty but pleasant smelling wheat poured into the hold from a swivelling spout which could be directed from the deck so that the flowing grain would fill up the less accessible places under the deck without the need to use a trimming shovel. The skipper decided we were going to take as much as it was possible to cram in. Wheat is not a particularly dense cargo and however much we managed to squeeze in we would still have a foot of freeboard. We got out the side cloths which we wedged into the battens on the coamings and laid along the decks, then, when the main hold was full, we put hatches on their sides just inside the coamings all round the hatchway and allowed the wheat to pour inside these temporary walls, finally rounding off the top of the heap. The remaining hatches we laid on the stack of wheat and drew the side cloths over so that they overlapped by several feet in the middle, then lashed the whole thing, criss cross, with a thin line fixed to rings outside the coamings. The same trick was repeated with the forehold, and thus we stowed the absolute maximum quantity of wheat that we could possibly accommodate. Once again the foot of the mainsail had to be tied up to clear the stack. The more we carried, the more we earned — ship and crew.

It was dark by the time we'd finished covering up. I lit the navigation lamps in the fo'c'sle, brought them on deck and the skipper fixed them into position. We had to heave the barge all the way to the dock entrance by trackline, but once out in the river a strong westerly wind took charge and we set all sail and went bowling away with the ebb, past Gravesend all the way to Southend and then we met the incoming tide. There was enough wind, however, to carry over the flood and we continued out into the Swin keeping close to the edge of the Maplin Sand away from the worst flow of the tide, going through the Spitway on the high water — to carry a new ebb nicely down to Harwich. We anchored on the Guard to wait for water into Felixstowe Dock over on the other side of the main fairway.

The wind was still blowing hard, but at least it was fair for the dock, and when we entered just before high water there was pandemonium aboard, because everything had to happen at once. Things on that occasion would have been easier with a crew of four. But there was only the skipper and me. He found it necessary to keep quite a lot of sail on the barge to get into the dock before being carried up river by the last of the flood; we sailed fast through the entrance, and swept on into the dock keeping well over to the starboard side. The skipper spun the wheel hard to port and cried out: *"Down tops'l, leggo the fores'l, brail up the mains'l, leggo the anchor!"* — all this in less time than it takes to write it down! I leaped from one rope to another, casting off halliards, letting topsail and foresail fall where they would, and frantically winding the handle on the brail winch. *"I said leggo the anchor!"* bawled the skipper, who was busy slacking off the main sheet. *"Awlright!"* I snarled back (under my breath, of course), racing up forward to throw chain over the windlass. Away went the anchor, dragging fifteen fathoms of chain after it. Suddenly everything was still and peaceful: we were within the shelter of the dock, lying quietly to our anchor, head to wind, our stern just clear of the concrete slipway at the end of the basin. I sagged against the bittheads to get my breath back and sucked a slightly torn finger, pinched by the anchor chain. Then the skipper was down in the boat sculling round the barge to take the end of the trackline from the bow across to the flour mill where a man on the quayside was waiting to make it fast. Back on board the skipper helped me get the anchor up, then we hove on the dolly winch and got ourselves alongside and tied up before high water.

I wonder if we called that evening at the Little Ships where they used to serve the most delicious sausage rolls anywhere on the East Coast; maybe not; it had been a tiring old passage, and there was still work to be done getting the hold uncovered for unloading. But we'd earned ourselves a little money.

Chapter Four

Coronation Race Day

1953 was Coronation Year. The old Thames and Medway Race Committees decided to hold one last sailing barge match in honour of the occasion. These races had been held in the Thames since 1863. Barges varied tremendously in their speed, and pre-war owners of the faster craft were tremendously proud of them, cossetting and titivating them all the year round in preparation for the great day. There was a rule that all the vessels competing must have carried cargo during the previous twelve months. To comply, some of the champion barges carried a mere one or two token freights and then only clean, lightweight cargoes.

When this, the last race of all was announced some owners withdrew their best barges from work, put them on the shipyard, refitted, painted, polished and generally fussed over them until they were a wonder to behold. I believe even the less pretentious barges spent two or three weeks previous to the race dried out somewhere to have the hull painted and dressed for a smoother, more slippery surface, and to mend sails and renew any suspect running rigging. Not so the *Clara*. We couldn't afford to lose a single freight, and had discharged a load of cement into a ship in Tilbury docks two days before the race. The next day we moored to a buoy off Gravesend and did what we could to make the old barge neat and tidy. Each craft competing in the restricted staysail class (ours) was allowed a crew of four; but champion bowsprits were allowed five. Our extra crew came on board that night. And then the skipper made his big mistake. He decided to lie overnight on the buoy off Gravesend. If, instead, he'd sailed away that evening, down to within a couple of cables of the starting line, and anchored *there* until morning, we wouldn't have made the disastrous start we did. Although we were up and away very early on the morning of the race, there was absolutely no wind; and by the time we had drifted down to the Lower Hope, where the committee steamer *Royal Sovereign* lay at the starting line, we were just about the last barge across. More fortunate barges had tugs to tow them to the line. Conditions remained calm all the way down Sea Reach, and the spare hand was kept busy throwing buckets of seawater at the mainsail — a practice intended to gain best advantage from any breath of air there was. In the end they decided to shorten the course and the turning point was just below Southend Pier. A breeze from the east came up with the afternoon flood, not long after we'd rounded the committee boat, but we remained at the tail end of the fleet all the way home, despite the skipper's cunning in taking advantage of currents and catspaws. We were not actually the last to arrive at the finishing line, but this was only because the *Glenmore* had broken her topmast! However, we were back at the Denton anchorage in time for the Supper (held in a posh hotel, the Clarendon Royal at Gravesend), which I enjoyed very much. I remember the roast chicken, the glass of wine and the animated conversations, speeches, and of course the presentations to the winners. The poor *Clara* was not among them. Each member of the crews, however, received a pewter tankard and a very handsome bronze medal to commemorate the event. I still have the medal to treasure but the tankard has been lost in the course of my many changes of address.

Chapter Five

Goodbye, Old *Clara*

SOON after the Coronation Barge Race the *Clara* sailed round to Maldon where she lay on Cook's shipyard blocks to be fitted with an engine. The skipper would very much have liked a Kelvin 44 h.p. which at that time was in fashion. But he couldn't afford it. Instead he settled for a 38 h.p. standard type road vehicle engine (was it a Ford?) which was converted and geared for marine use by Parsons at Southampton.

Usually ships' engines are set amidships and as far aft as possible, but in converting a sailing barge the engine had to be positioned to one side of the kelson to avoid the enormous wooden sternpost and the rudder. So the ceiling on the starboard side at the forward end of the *Clara's* main cabin was taken up and engine beds constructed and fitted into the bilge to take the weight of the machinery. A hole had to be drilled through the quarter to accommodate the stern tube and shaft. Cooks set a very elderly shipwright (accompanied by an equally elderly dog) to the task, and he did it all by hand; there were no electric tools at the yard at that time. By some magical means he calculated where he had to start on the outside and where the auger would emerge on the inside. It was a long and tedious operation, involving, I should think, many hundreds of turns of the auger. The resulting hole wasn't just straight through a three inch thickness of plank, but slanted at a very fine angle through a massive oak log which had been fastened to the hull. A second auger enlarged the original hole, and that in its turn was still further enlarged by a third — until the tunnel measured some 2½ inches diameter.

We manhandled the engine below and bolted it to the new beds, ran a rod through the stern tube and — horror! Not only would the shaft come out half an inch too high, it would also be half an inch to one side. The skipper was in despair until a friend of his stepped aboard to see how we were getting on. Sometimes this man had sailed as a voluntary spare hand on the *Clara* and indeed had been one of our racing crew, and as a lover of pure sail his attitude towards the engine was unenthusiastic. However, instead of scoffing at our distress he decided to take the matter in hand. Now, thirty years on, he has contributed the following passage to my narrative.

"The appearance at Maldon of my old friend the *Clara* was always pleasing, though on one occasion my pleasure was tinged with sadness for I heard from the skipper that he was now proposing to get into the fashion by installing a small auxiliary engine. I had known for some months that he was dreaming up something of that kind, but his early thinking had run more on the lines of a large outboard — of the kind they were experimenting with on the Chelmer and Blackwater Canal barges. His declared policy was to defeat the loadline regulations which limited the small locally owned auxiliaries to the River Thames smooth water area, and forbade them to proceed below Colne Point in winter and Clacton in summer. His greatest concern was to keep open the lucrative Ipswich option which would be denied him unless he went to great expense with an inboard auxiliary. These ideas came to nothing. What he finally settled for was an inexpensive, marinised lorry engine — I believe from the Southampton firm of Parsons — and thereby the consequent smooth water restrictions.

"In spite of my sadness I had to admit to myself that the days of the pure sailing barges were over. It was all very fine for a handful of dreamers still in their teens or early twenties to cling to the romantic notion of commercial sail; indeed at that moment I was myself in the process of creating a charitable organisation whose aim was to keep a barge trading in perpetuity under sail alone. But for an older man with responsibilities on shore and the desire for a less onerous life afloat, there could be nothing but benefit in the post war fashion of auxiliary power — and the ultimate goal no doubt of full motorisation of the coasting fleet.

"At first though I was disposed to show nothing but scorn and derision. But soon it became pitifully clear that all was not going well with my friend's plans and that in all probability he would find himself in the bankruptcy court long before he could make the new engine start to pay for itself. The shipwrights had laid the engine beds and completed the slow operation of boring for the stern tube. The engine had arrived on board and was being set up on its beds. A second-hand propeller had been obtained, also an A-bracket, but there was no tube — and most significantly, no shaft.

"The war had been over nine years, but its debilitating effects on industry were still powerfully felt — nowhere more so than in the field of engineering. It happened that I was an engineer's buyer, and the great burden of my working life was the never-ending problem of obtaining enough raw steel products to keep 800 men employed. I knew very well that the skipper might as well have asked for gold as for the random length of two-inch stainless steel that he needed for his shaft, and decided that I had better see what could be done to relieve the situation. After many days and a small fortune in telephone calls, I succeeded in locating a suitable piece of solid drawn Admiralty brass tube; but it seemed that in all the length and breadth of the British Isles there was not a single length of turned and polished stainless steel shafting. Eventually after applying to just about every steel manufacturer and stockholder in the Kingdom, I managed to run to earth a length of two-inch round black stainless steel bar 'as drawn', and had it brought post haste by road to Heybridge Works.

"The turnery foreman shook his head as it lay in his shop to be tapered and threaded for the propeller: 'I don't think *that* will do for a boat. It'd need to be skimmed, and we haven't a lathe to accommodate such a length.'

"Seeing my consternation, however, he decided to call an emergency meeting — of the toolroom manager, and the most experienced of Bentall's lathe operators. Between them they worked something out. My friend, the cost office manager, the son of a Maldon fisherman, turned a blind eye to the quite staggering sum of money involved in making up special tools and fittings for the lathe — which, if charged, would certainly have bankrupted the poor old *Clara!*

"As soon as the stern tube was inserted in its tunnel we saw that our troubles were far from over, for it was an inch out of line in both planes! The poor skipper was on the verge of tears. 'This'll be the finish of me!' he groaned. And certainly it did look very much that way.

"Now, I do not profess to be an engineer; but those problematical years with E H Bentall & Company had taught me just a little about improvisation. 'A universal joint will be the thing,' I said with an impressive show of youthful confidence. 'It's no good,' the skipper cried. 'A universal joint can only correct part of the fault.'

" 'Then it will have *two* universal joints,' I replied breezily — and dashed off up to the town to see the Commodore of my yacht club who owned the garage in the High Street. The Commodore was mightily amused. 'It's never been done before, that's certain!' he laughed. 'But there's no reason I can see why it shouldn't work. Give me a couple of hours. . . .'

"Later that day I returned and found the gadget waiting for me. 'Tell them to be careful the first few times they chuck her in and out of gear; I've put a piece of splined shaft under the weld so it should be OK; but tell him not to run at it like a bull at a gate and expect to go from full ahead to full astern — just in case!' (In those days everyone in Maldon knew something useful about a boat.)

"The local engineers who were helping with the installation, were sorely dubious; but their doubts were quickly brushed aside by the skipper. 'It'll *work!*' he said, full, once more, of old familiar optimism. 'In years to come everybody will have one of these. We're going to take out a patent; we'll end up millionaires!'

"The job was almost finished; it now remained to find a length of copper tube to lead from the engineroom to the outside stern gear for purpose of lubrication. No more than a couple of hours' work to fit.

" 'Three-eighths bore copper tube? Certainly, sir, six months delivery. . . .'

"Again consternation on the face of the engineer. Not so with the skipper: 'This man does miracles to order!' he said, with that incorrigible old grin of his. He meant me of course. So I got into the works car and drove to Ipswich — straight to the chief engineer of the Manganese Bronze and Brass Company.

" 'Oilite bearings. Will they work in seawater?'

"A conference was quickly convened in the Chief Designer's office. After a great deal of discussion somebody said: 'Why not? We admit we don't actually know; but why shouldn't they work perfectly well under water? We'll supply the bushes if you'll give them a test — no charge of course.' Oilite is a magical substance — sintered bronze or brass, reconstituted with the addition of oil. A 'bush' (or plain bearing) made from oilite never needed to be lubricated. At our works we were using the things all the time; two-inch bore was a standard size; there were hundreds in the warehouse.

"As I waved the *Clara* goodbye, the skipper shouted: 'I shall have to report you, you know, to the Royal Society for the Preservation of Sail. We'll visit you in Chelmsford prison, next time we're down!'

"Against improbable odds the freak universal joint was a complete success and served the *Clara* well for what remained of her working days. Of the life of the oilite bearings under water I regret I can say nothing, but perhaps the Manganese Bronze people (are they still there?) went ahead with some tests of their own. It would be a great luxury to me not to have to go below to my own reeking engine-room every couple of hours to turn the handles on the stern greasers!"

*   *   *

Clara went on the blocks at Maldon a sailing barge, and she came off an auxiliary. We left the mizzen ashore, though we motor-sailed about for a while. Still we were without any shelter for the steersman, such as the other auxiliary barges were beginning to enjoy. Then the skipper decided that we too should have one. First of all it was a three-sided box with window frames but no roof, though on occasions of heavy rain we dragged a piece of tarpaulin over the frame to keep out the worst of the wet. I don't believe it was ever actually finished.

We had a regular, long-term, contract to carry ballast into Leigh on Sea (just up the river from Southend). As ever, it was a most awkward, chancy place to try to get a deep loaded barge into. It was bad enough in daylight: on the big spring tides we could approach the wharf in a more or less direct line from the south-east; on poor tides we had to keep to the meandering creek, some of the corners of which were marked with thin stakes maintained there by the local fishermen.

But, as ever, poor us! most often it was dark and we evolved a system which brought us from seaward to a point off the railway station at Westcliff by lining up the lights on certain prominent features on the shore. We usually lay at anchor there until half an hour before high water when we would generally feel our way through a small fleet of yachts and dinghies on moorings, and I would stand up forward sounding the water with a long boathook which had been painted in foot-wide stripes, black and white, feeling for the sudden deep water of the extremely narrow creek — upon reaching which the barge was steered quickly at right angles to proceed along the creek to the wharf.

We managed to honour this contract for many months, but one night the inevitable happened. On a poor tide I was too long finding the creek with the pole; the tide perhaps started to recede early, and we grounded athwart the creek and were unable to back off. In this compromising position the *Clara* dried out and broke her back. We had to leave her there until the tides started to increase and she was towed into Leigh to be discharged. Thus the *Clara* ended her trading life and was sold off as some sort of clubhouse in the upper reaches of the Thames.

Chapter Six

Off to Sea in a Motor Barge

CONTRARY to my father's prediction, I stayed working on the water for fourteen years, all that time with the same skipper. In many respects he was an unusual type of bargeman. He possessed a superior intellect and was an omnivorous and insatiable reader. His preference was for solid biography and history, but he was prepared to read anything that lay at hand, (like myself), right down to the label on the marmalade jar at breakfast time. Once we took a load of pulp to a paper mill in Erith on the River Thames, and found ourselves lying alongside a lighter full of old books for pulping. It was a veritable Aladdin's cave; we'd be there still if they hadn't come and taken the lighter away! We each gathered up an armful of the nearest books that took our fancy — torn, damp, and backless as many of them were. They kept us quiet for a long time; when they were finished, we often thought longingly of all the others lost to us in the pulping factory.

The skipper had a modest vocabulary of Latin, and often used such words quite naturally in ordinary conversation. I knew none at all, and for a long time thought that they were nonsense words he had made up (I believe his pronunciation was highly individual). Then one day I heard a phrase on the radio that he often used, and realised the truth of the matter.

It seemed to me that there was nothing he could not do when he turned his hand to it. With the aid of the engine manual he could strip down, find a fault, rectify it, and reassemble any of the engines we ever had — from a 250 h.p. Blackstone down to the little two-stroke Anzani outboard. He would do any carpentry work needed aboard, though I believe he admitted to not being much of a cabinet maker! He knew about compass adjusting and also the mysteries of electricity and spent much time, vainly, in trying to get me to understand those subjects. He could also mend any odd bits of small machinery such as our typewriter and the little sewing machine I kept aboard; all I'd need to do was tell him what seemed to be malfunctioning; he'd study it intently for a minute then: "Ah yes, I think if I just . . ." and with a screwdriver and

37

No Paper Mill at Erith — must be Thames Board Mill at Purfleet a small spanner he'd be able to locate the fault and put it right for me.

If he had a fault, in my eyes, (or rather to my ears), it was that he was utterly tone deaf and couldn't carry any tune. Every tune, he used to claim, sounded like God Save the King (if it was slow) or Good King Wenceslas (if it was fast)! Many times when we were in the wheelhouse together, on a long passage, I would try to teach him the tonic sol fa, and though he could *say* the names of the notes, he could never sing beyond doh, ray, me — after which his voice went falsetto and he got the names in the wrong order. It was frustrating.

We only had two serious differences of opinion that remained for ever unresolved. He reckoned the blunt end of a boiled egg should be fitted into the egg-cup, whereas I always fitted the pointed end; and where those alphabetical dividers are fitted into correspondence files, *he* said that the papers to be filed should go in front of the appropriate divider, and *I* (and surely the rest of the commercial world) put them behind the divider. . . .

I never heard him utter the popular expletives in constant use by everybody we came in contact with in our working environment. Indeed he didn't seem to need any of the normal swear words, for he had his own highly individual style of eloquence for relieving frustration. He was tall and strong and hard-working and to my mind overtaxed that strength when he lifted a large bronze propeller from the ground to fit to the end of the propeller shaft, perhaps straining his heart as a result, and bringing about his untimely death, some years ago, at the age of sixty.

After losing the *Clara* the skipper and I were out of work for a while. Then he found work for us with the firm of Samuel West who owned several auxiliary and fully powered barges, most of them engaged in the ballast work between the Colne and the Thames and Medway. We spent a month in that work (gaining valuable experience for what was to come later), and were eventually given charge of the *Olive May*.

She was West's largest vessel, her massive timbers capable of carrying 200 tons. With her we found a much wider field of operations, extending as far north as Blyth in Northumberland and south-west as far as Par in Cornwall. Built originally as a sailing barge, by now she had had all the sailing gear removed, and was trading under power. Though no ocean greyhound, the *Olive May* was to me matchless for her easy steering. When we were on a long straight course we could lash the wheel with a piece of rope to an eye-bolt set into the floor of the wheelhouse, and she would maintain her course untouched for as long as we needed to keep it.

For the long coasting passages undertaken at this period, the *Olive May* was reckoned a three-handed craft. The London office, however took no interest in supplying a third hand so we obtained a succession of young lads from employment exchanges in various ports — kids who'd never been afloat and thought they might like it, and who usually, after one trip, (or even half a trip), never wanted to be afloat again. One we got from Ipswich after loading scrap metal for Middlesbrough. He came aboard just before we sailed, clutching a paper carrier bag containing apparently everything he thought he might need while away from home for possibly several weeks at a time. When finally we arrived at Redcar Jetty at the mouth of the Tees (in those days before the North Sea oil platform era a bleak place, deserted and remote from human habitation or transport facilities), I caught a temporary turn round a pile, and in a flash the boy was up the ladder, the carrier bag between his teeth, across the jetty and was last seen running in the direction of the flat horizon, shouting over his shoulder: "Send my money on!"

The skipper used the phone on the jetty to get our berthing orders, but he came back with the news that there wasn't yet a berth for us up at Middlesbrough, and he was to phone again next day. Meantime we could lie where we were because no ore carrier was due for some days. Next morning on the phone again. Still no berth. We were getting low on grub and the skipper hadn't seen a newspaper for a couple of days (a privation which always made him feel faint). So we put the lifeboat over the side, shipped out trusty Anzani, and set off up the river the few miles to Middlesbrough's civilisation. We didn't need to use the outboard engine going that way, because we had the flood tide and a strong breeze from the east. I sat up forward and used the skipper's large black umbrella as a spinnaker, while he steered with an oar over the stern. We made a very swift passage (and a cheap one for us, who had to buy our own petrol for the outboard), to Middlesbrough — causing much astonishment and pointing among the natives as we sped past the wharves in the upper reaches.

Middlesbrough was the place, on another occasion, where a distressing thing happened to my skipper. We had brought in a load of what he called "bowings and scrapings" actually borings and scrap tins: the tins were compressed into large cubes and weighed light for their bulk; borings were those fragments of metal that result from the machining of metal parts and were very heavy for their bulk — half a bucketful

was as much as I could lift. Our method of loading the cargo was to
have the crane dump two piles in the middle of the main hold until we
were well down in our marks, and the rest of the space in the hold
would be filled with scrap tins. Sometimes we filled the side decks with
further blocks of compressed tins, thereby increasing the freight. On
the present occasion the barge was being unloaded and the skipper set
off to the City taking with him the paperwork for the ship's agent.
(Whenever we loaded or unloaded at Middlesbrough there was always
a long walk to the City, and we used to swear it always rained when we
were there.) At the conclusion of his business the skipper set out to
walk back to the ship and on the way his shoes fell to pieces. That was
the story he told me. It seems he was outside a shoeshop when this
happened, and entered in his stockinged feet, so demoralised (he
explained) that the salesman was able quite easily to sell him a pair of
shoes made by Thomas Tricker — one of the most expensive makes of
footwear in the shop. Of those shoes he was to remain inordinately
proud for many years.

*   *   *

It was from Middlesbrough that we set off to load coal at Blyth. This
was a passage of about forty miles; we didn't put the hatches on after
unloading, just the beams with the lifeboat perched somewhat pre-
cariously on top, most of its weight still held by the derrick. It seemed a
fine enough day when we set out from Middlesbrough. The radio
forecast indicated a light south-easterly breeze which suited us well
enough. We motored away in high spirits; but as soon as we were clear
of the long pier at the mouth of the Tees we found there was an
uncomfortable swell from the south-east, and the breeze steadily
increasing to a moderate gale.

We headed north-west with the seas behind us, hurrying past and
lifting high into the air, surging on ahead and leaving our stern in the
trough — to be lifted again by a successor. The swell is very short
indeed in the North Sea, but the *Olive May* was a joy to steer, light or
loaded (except when trimmed by the head). She didn't greatly object
to being grabbed by the tail, lifted up, stood on her head then dropped
into a deep hole; and to tell the truth her crew rather enjoyed the roller
coaster ride as far as the mouth of the Tyne. Running before the wind
and sea I didn't appreciate the strength of those elements until we met
a large collier coming out of Seaham Harbour deep loaded and most
likely bound for London. How ponderously she plunged her stem into

the depths, as if she was going to continue straight to the bottom, picking up again, pointing her nose at the sky and wallowing into the next trough. I was horrified as I watched. But we fairly flew past her and soon she was nothing but masts and a funnel, disappearing on the lumpy horizon far astern.

Darkness fell, and the skipper had to decide what to do next. He said it didn't do to try for Blyth harbour entrance in the dark with a south-easterly gale, and the next shelter after that being the Firth of Forth, our best plan would be to try for a berth in the Tyne. Entry here was also quite tricky in the conditions prevailing, so he called up the Tyne pilots on the RT to ask permission to lie inside the river for the night — and please could we have a pilot to assist us in? The cutter came out to put a pilot aboard, and he saw us safely between the north and south piers and found us a mooring buoy off South Shields where we lay the night in perfect comfort.

By the morning the weather had fined away and we were able to nip out of the Tyne, round the corner into Blyth Harbour, and load our coal for Exeter. A very quick, efficient loading system there; above the wharf a railway carried trucks which tipped sideways allowing the coal to cascade down chutes into the barge. When the main hold was getting full, men came aboard with enormous triangular shovels and with the utmost economy and commendable speed shifted the top of the heap into the wings underneath the side decks until the *Olive May* was full to her marks. The skipper always claimed he couldn't understand any English spoken north of Great Yarmouth; he called down to the cabin for me to come up to interpret what the Blyth trimmers were saying, when they wanted us to move. They must have thought it very peculiar. At that time we had no third hand. After we left Blyth we began to experience a lot of trouble with the engine. I believe we put into every other port on the East Coast — Bridlington, Yarmouth, Brightlingsea — each time getting some local engineer to come to our aid. At Brightlingsea they said the engine was indeed in a parlous state, but they did at least get us going again. We picked up a third hand there — an ex pig farmer who thought he'd like to go to sea.

Three days later we arrived off Exmouth. It was midnight. In calm conditions we felt able to drop the anchor and await a pilot for Exeter next morning. But at 7 a.m. a strong swell was rolling in from the south, even though there was no wind; the pilot station advised us by radio that they were sending out the cutter immediately and would we please up anchor and be ready to leave, for there was some nasty weather on the way. We knew better than to raise the anchor until we had got our troublesome engine started, so the skipper disappeared into the engine-room to inquire how it was feeling this fine day? Not co-operative. It needed to be started by compressed air, of which there were two cylinders, both full. All this was soon used up without a single cough from the engine. The compressor was started, to recharge the empty air bottles and further attempts made to start the works. Nothing doing. This procedure was continued for half an hour by which time the donkey engine had started to overheat. We led a hosepipe down from the deck, through the engine-room skylight, to the top of the donkey, a funnel was inserted in the deck end of the pipe and I was kept busy pouring buckets of sea water down to keep the compressor engine cool. The skipper, as soon as there was enough air in the bottle, applied it, fruitlessly, to the main engine.

In the meantime the pilot boat had arrived from Exmouth and was hovering close by, tossing up and down like a demented rocking horse. I took a short break from dousing the donkey to walk up forward to feel the anchor chain to see if the anchor was holding. It wasn't holding. In fact I didn't have to touch the bar taut chain to feel the vibration of a dragging anchor; I could actually hear it scraping along the rocky bottom as I stood there on the plunging fo'c'sle head. I passed this unwelcome news down to the skipper; he acknowledged with a nod of the head: "I'll come up and have a look in a minute," he said. I went on dipping up water and pouring it down over the hot little donkey, and skipper made two more attempts at starting the other machinery — still without success. Then he looked up at me through the skylight as I was about to pour the umpteenth bucket down the hosepipe, shook his head and made the motion of breaking a stick in half, indicating complete failure of the engine. I put the bucket down and he came up on deck to view the scene which had altered a lot since last he surveyed it.

There was a strong wind southerly, and the seas were rolling, short and steep, from the direction of the Bay of Biscay. The sky was blue and the sun shone brilliantly, the sea pale green streaked with foam as the tops of the waves collapsed. But it wasn't a time to be admiring the beauty of the scene: as we dragged along the bottom, the red cliffs of Devon loomed inexorably larger and we could see the breakers crashing on to the rocks. The skipper gave out another few fathoms of chain which brought us up sharply — but only for a moment; soon we could hear the grrrrumble, grrrumble of the anchor along the bottom. The pilot boat, a mere cockle-shell about fifteen feet long with a tiny box of a wheelhouse and three men on board, crossed our head and passed close down the starboard side.

"Engine broken down," the skipper shouted.

"Do you want us to try and tow you in?" came the reply.

"Lloyds rules," the skipper stipulated.

"Aye, Lloyds rules," was the answer.

Then he turned to me. "We're getting a bit close, lass; do you want to transfer to the pilot boat?" I compared the dancing boatlet nearby with the relatively stable and solid barge beneath my feet and shook my head. The skipper nodded and said we must get ready with our best rope for the tow. This was a long, unbroken and nearly new length of eight-inch coir, very light, springy and buoyant. We uncoiled it aft and ran it along the middle of the hatchway to get rid of the kinks, tying a large bowline on the forward end. The pilot boat, having run right round behind us, came down the starboard side again and the skipper tossed them a heaving line. I attached the bowline of the tow rope to the heaving line and it was hauled aboard the pilot boat and made fast. We led it through the snatch on the starboard bowrail, then made it fast on a deck bollard. The pilot boat left sufficient slack in the rope for us to heave up the anchor, and as soon as the chain was up and down, indicating that the anchor was off the bottom, they motored ahead, leading our tow rope abeam instead of ahead. The next sea that hit us seemed to lift the barge's head right out of the water and as we crashed into the following trough, the jerk carried away the snatch and part of the wooden bow rail. But the rope and the bollard both held, and with the tow rope leading direct from the bollard over the broken rail, the pilot boat again began to forge ahead. I suppose from the shore we must have resembled a large, fat lady being taken for a walk by a small, frisky terrier dog. The entrance into the River Exe is taken at an angled C; straight from the sea to the blank wall of a cliff, a sharp left turn, continue parallel to the shore for a few hundred yards, turn sharp right and you're in the river; then right again and you're into Exmouth Harbour, safe and sound. Under tow, it didn't happen quite like that. We were a heavy load for the poor little pilot boat to manage, and to keep from piling up on the rocks the *Olive May* crabbed sideways along each leg of the course, until eventually all was accomplished and we were brought sweetly to rest at a nice solid stone quay inside Exmouth Harbour. We learned that the pilot boat radioed to the lifeboat station to stand by in case of emergency: this had been noted with interest by holidaymakers. There was a large crowd about the harbour waiting to see what would happen. The contrast between our former state, the wind, the sea, the shining rocks and the flying spray outside, and the beautiful warm, calm, sunny atmosphere of the harbour — between the shirt-sleeved and cotton-dressed holiday crowds, the children in their scanty bathing dress, and the bedraggled, soaking wet crew of the *Olive May*!

"Rough out there was it?" a bystander inquired as we were tying up at the quay.

"Ooh, a bit rough," the skipper confessed. He was not a man much given to sailorly exaggeration.

Then the crews of the pilot boat and the *Olive May* retired to the nearest pub and had a drink — or was it two? Our Brightlingsea engineers were sent for. When they arrived and got the engine stripped down, they quickly identified our trouble. The reason she wouldn't start was simple: three of the six pistons were cracked, and all the rings broken!

*   *   *

It was on a later run down Channel that my skipper gave us all such a fright. We had unloaded coal at Newport, Isle of Wight and our next orders were for Par in Cornwall and a freight of china clay for the Medway. You will understand that as coal is black, dusty and gritty, and china clay is soft, sticky and white as snow, to have to load the latter immediately after discharging the former must entail a certain amount of hard labour and a few harsh words among the crew. After the coal was discharged the crew had to sweep up the leavings and transfer them by bucket from the hold into the ship's domestic coal bunker; and any little bits hiding behind protruding frames and knees, and any dust lurking on top of the nuts and bolts (scores of them), or in cracks in the lining, ceiling and deck head — all had to be sought out, brushed down and swept up. The skipper explained to the dusty mate and third hand that before we could take on china clay, the loading manager would come down into the hold and roll a ball of it from one end to the other, and if the clay showed the smallest contamination he would request that the sweeping and scrubbing be repeated before any loading could begin. So we were kept there, sweeping and dusting, worse than a Tyneside housewife.

Our subsequent passage down Channel was made in the night. It was flat calm and bright moonlight, so once again we didn't trouble to put the hatches and tarpaulin over the hold, just the beams with the lifeboat perched on top, some of the weight taken up on the lifting strop. In the middle of the night, the skipper's watch, the third hand (not the pig farmer — he went straight back from Exmouth to his pigs — this one was a lad from Suffolk) and the mate were turned in. When under way I used to snooze on the day bed in the saloon beneath the wheelhouse, for immediate readiness if needed. On this occasion I was most rudely awaked by the extraordinary corkscrew motion of the ship; being practically thrown from the sofa, where I was lying fully dressed except for shoes with a blanket tucked round me. Hastily disentangling myself from the blanket, I lurched about searching for my shoes, colliding painfully with the saloon table. When I had stumbled up the three steps to the wheelhouse the skipper was the only calm thing in sight amid the general pandemonium. The ship was pitching and rolling crazily and the mast describing wide circles against the moonlit sky; the seas looked as steep and as high as the Pyramids, leaping and tossing in all directions, malevolently trying, only a little short of success, to capsize the poor old *Olive May*. The ill-secured lifeboat just about to break loose from the hatchway, the stays of the mast alternately slacking and twanging taut. I felt that I had never been closer to shipwreck. And yet, in all this, there still wasn't a breath of wind! "Crikey!" I said, "What's happening?"

"Oh, I thought I'd just edge us into the Portland Race to speed us along," the skipper said, with monumental nonchalance. "But I think it's just a bit too much of a good thing, don't you? Sorry I woke you. Hold on to the wheel for a moment, while I nip out and subdue the lifeboat." When he'd thrown a rope across the boat and tied it firmly down, he came back inside the wheelhouse and said: "OK, back you go and finish your sleep." But of course I was now wide awake. Once we were clear of the Race we proceeded more sedately down Channel. I made a cup of coffee and we shared the rest of the watch. Daylight saw our arrival off Par, where the sea is coloured the most lovely milky turquoise by the china clay effluent washed down from the quarries inland. Actually it wasn't precisely Par where we were to load, but at the neat little double harbour nearby called Charlestown. Unless I misremember, we entered the tiny outer harbour between two curved stone walls and then went through a lock gate into an even tinier saucer of a harbour. There we lay under a chute from which fell lumps of ice-white clay. Before they started loading, sure enough down into the hold came a man to examine it for cleanliness, but he did it merely by eye; we were down in the hold with him gazing apprehensively, willing him not to make us sweep the hold again. He frowned slightly, but in the end didn't say a word, and we were thankful to see the loading begin.

It was on the voyage back to the Medway, when we rode out a strong wind in the lee of the Isle of Wight that we discovered that the third hand had thrown overboard all the loaves of bread we had in stock, because, he said, they were stale! This put him in very bad odour with the skipper and with me; I suppose I must have spoken unkindly to him, because he took umbrage and refused to work from then on. When we reached Rochester a couple of days later, by that time hungry enough to eat the third hand, my skipper discharged him there even though the barge was bound a good way further up the river to the paper mill near Maidstone.

We carried our tide up to the berth at the factory, made all fast and prepared the ship for unloading the following morning. It was then six in the evening.

"Come on," said the skipper, "we'll get a bus into Maidstone and find something to eat." So we did, and by some magic chance (for neither of us had ever been to Maidstone before) we came upon a hotel called (and I'll never forget the name) the Blue Star, where we had the most fabulous meal. It was the sort of place where the waiter wheels up a large trolley crowded on two levels with dishes of hors d'oeuvres, piles up your plate until you are ashamed — and that was only for starters. After there was steak and kidney pie and after that . . . well it was one of those meals which occasion: "Do you remember . . ." remarks for years to come, whenever the subject of food arises.

Chapter Seven

A Freight to the Norfolk Broads

DURING our two years in the *Olive May* we must have called into every port both large and small on the East and South coasts of England. Sometimes delivering or collecting freight, but probably more often because of engine trouble or bad weather (or even both). Bridlington was the great favourite, being the last place to shelter before rounding Flamborough Head when bound northward. It was a dry-out harbour and always had a berth available for us on its long quay. Once when lying there windbound, on the way to Middlesbrough, the skipper and I walked round to the coastguard tower at the tip of Flamborough and climbed the wooden steps to chat with the guard on watch. There was an anemometer outside the tower and we watched the dial in the office reading about 30 knots, which must occasion hoisting a storm cone on the tower's mast. Through the coastguard's telescope we watched with a delicious sensation of horror some collier or deep sea trawler ploughing doggedly into the seas which swept them from end to end.

On another occasion we were in Bridlington with the usual engine trouble and waiting for a new part to come by train. It was a lovely day and as the tide was high, the skipper launched the lifeboat, shipped the outboard engine and we ventured outside the harbour to troll for mackerel. We each had a line with a spinner at the end; with the outboard just ticking over we paraded up and down outside the pierhead. In a short time the skipper had a catch, hauled it in, removed the hook from its mouth and quickly had the line back in the water. Then I caught one, and hauled it in. But I had never taken hold of a living fish to remove a hook and I looked at it flapping about on the bottom boards — and recoiled at the prospect. I asked the skipper to remove the hook for me. "I'm busy!" he snapped hauling in another fish. "Don't be silly, take it off the hook at once!"

I usually try to do what I'm ordered, so gingerly I grasped it round its middle and removed the hook as gently as I could, quickly dropping the fish back on to the bottom boards and leaving it there to gasp out

47

the remainder of its life. After that, of course, I thought nothing of it. In ten minutes we had ten large mackerel in the boat. We returned to the ship, and within half an hour four of them had been beheaded, gutted, split and fried and were on our plates. They were quite delicious (free food again!). We finished them off for breakfast the following day. It's the only way; mackerel must be eaten freshly caught.

We never went into Whitby when bound northwards (if we could get that far we could go on to the Tees, a mere twenty miles further on); but quite often we used that pretty little harbour for shelter when trying to get south. In this case it was the last haven (except for Scarborough which wasn't so easy) before rounding Flamborough. If we sheltered in Whitby there could be a south cone visible on the mast at the entrance. At Whitby there is an outer harbour, then round a corner a smaller inner harbour, both usually crowded with fishing vessels of many nationalities and of all sizes from the little local coble to quite large trawlers. As it was more comfortable we always went to the inner harbour, where we lay alongside the quay just across the road from Woolworths and Boots (very handy for me because I was a subscriber to Boots library and could change my books at any branch in the country — they don't have a library system now, more's the pity). During our visits we explored the town, looked round the Abbey and one day took the small boat upstream until it became too shallow. Whilst on the river we saw an enormous salmon leap out of the water almost near enough for us to catch — what a beauty he was — then he fell back into the water with a tremendous splash.

We got into Whitby late one evening, tied up at our customary berth with unusual despatch, and leapt ashore across the road into the nearest pub just in time for the last orders call. "Have you got anything to eat?" we inquired breathlessly. The landlord, though a bit dubious, thought he might be able to find us "a bit of something", and soon brought us two plates each containing a great hunk of home made pork pie with a splash of hot mustard alongside. We devoured it ravenously, washed it down with a pint (and a half pint) of beer, and afterwards declared it the best pie ever baked.

We had a love-hate relationship with the port of Great Yarmouth. We were glad enough of its being where it was, otherwise there would have been a very long stretch of coastline without shelter from the Humber to the Ipswich river. But it can be a place of great difficulty to enter. The skipper reckoned it was only safe to go in half an hour each

(12) Myself when young. When I first ran away to sea, it was still considered
unsuitable for a girl to wear trousers, and I worked in a skirt and jumper.
By the time of this photograph the *Clara* had lost her mizen and gained
an auxiliary engine. The winch under the boat davits was used to wind up
the heavy leeboards, and also had a useful warping barrel.

(14)   Approaching Alresford swing-bridge in ideal conditions. All too often it was dark/foggy/blowing hard/raining on my glasses. Not the most popular place for loading.

Left: (13)   The *Clara* alongside, ready for loading. These little ports were then, mercifully, free of yachts and of quayside spectators — and the few sailing barges remaining pursued their workaday trading almost unnoticed.

ft, top: (15) *Clara* loading ballast at Alresford.

below: (16) Our old friend *Centaur* at the Freshwater ballast jetty, Fingringhoe.

Above: (17) At the London end we usually loaded out of ocean-going ships. In the 1950s the Port of London was a very much busier place than it is now. The lighters which loaded with us were popular with the dockers; we 'sailormen' were not. They would be towed away for later discharge at up-river wharves; drifting unattended in the docks they obstructed our progress — a great nuisance.

(18) Three phases in the decline of the spritsail barge, taking place during my
years on the water: from one the mizzen and bowsprit are gone; from
another the topmast has gone; from the other two all sailing gear gone.
All four had workmanlike diesel engines.

(19) End of an era: the mighty *Hydrogen* motors by in a calm. Sometimes a sailing barge drifting helplessly would be given a helping hand.

(20) The end of the *Clara*. Athwart the creek bed at Leigh-on-Sea.

(21) Her last known resting place.

side of high or low water, in other words, in the slack of the tide. Long twin piers jut out from the land at right angles making for a narrow entrance. The approach is from east to west. If the tide is sluicing up or down, north to south or south to north, it is a struggle to get safely between the pierheads before the current sets the ship on top of one or the other of them. The short period of slack water is undoubtedly the best time to attempt entry. The worst combination of circumstances to be imagined is full ebb in a strong, or worse (but that is unthinkable!) easterly wind. Inevitably there was an occasion when we found ourselves in the position of having to enter under just those conditions. We were loaded with coal for Norwich and having rolled our way south from the Humber and arrived at Yarmouth Roads, we had but two choices: we could carry on up the coast and shelter in Harwich until the weather moderated. Or we could take our chance on getting into Yarmouth at half tide. We couldn't lie at anchor in the Roads until low water; the sea was too rough.

The skipper elected to try his luck. He told me I was to stand at the other side of the wheel from him, but not to take it until he told me to. We headed towards the entrance pointing the bow towards the end of the south pier (remember, the tide was sluicing out) with the engine on emergency power. When we were between the two piers the skipper put the wheel to starboard to line the barge up with the piers, whereupon the tide seized us beam on and started to rush us towards the north pier. So it was hard over with the wheel to port, the skipper's way, who then let it go, allowing the pressure of the rudder to spin it back to starboard. The skipper cried: "Stop her!" and I caught hold of it, being only just able to stop its frantic spin. And thus we made progress up between the piers, crabwise through short steep waves which were in chaotic disarray, contending with a brisk wind from the east and the full force of the tide from the south which rebounded from the piers to create a most horrible muddle. Despite the weather, which was cold and damp, there were many anglers fishing from the piers, each huddled blankly over his lifeless rod, and many spectators who had come to view the intense drama of a little ship battling her way to safety. The really difficult part could have lasted no more than a couple of minutes, then we were round the corner in the safety of the River Yare, and calm water. At the time I would have testified that our ordeal had lasted very much longer than that.

Next day, just after dawn, long before any of the holidaymakers were about in their sailing yachts and cruisers we stole quietly up the river towards the gas works at Norwich to discharge our coal. It was utterly still and silent except for the murmur of the engine below and the calls of a great variety of birds. There were wraiths of mist hanging over the reeds, making the whole scene utterly enchanting. Ships on the River Yare are required to proceed in either direction at their minimum speed. For one thing there is a bye-law aimed at preserving the river banks, and also the channel is sinuous, narrow and shallow, and a loaded vessel would not be easy to steer at any great speed, with only inches under the propeller. Occasionally our wheelhouse caught up in the willow trees overhanging the water's edge as we rounded a bend. In all, it was a pleasant change from our usual element, the grey, grim North Sea.

*   *   *

Our employment as Master and Mate of the *Olive May* was abruptly terminated one day when we were loading scrap metal at Colchester Hythe. We had done several freights from there to Middlesbrough, and the system was always the same. We would berth at the lower end of Colchester's Old Quay, facing down river, starboard side to the quay. The yard where the scrap metal was assembled lay a few steps from the edge of the quay, behind a containing wall. A mobile crane would trundle out of the yard, position itself at the edge of the wharf, pick up a grabful of scrap from the pile, swing the jib round and dump it into the hold. (When the heap in the hold became easily accessible from the deck, the mate could be seen sorting through it, looking for bits of brass and copper which we collected, and when we had a small sackful sold it to a non-ferrous metal merchant — one of our very few perks.)

Industrial cranes of all types have a safe working load indicator with a pointer on a dial to indicate how much weight has been picked up and is suspended from the end of the jib. When the safe working load is exceeded, a bell rings loudly — a warning of danger. On the occasions that we loaded at this wharf the warning bell seemed to sound every time the grab picked up a load, but nobody took any notice. On this day we had started loading in the morning, and after breakfast I plodded up into the town to buy supplies for the voyage. When I had finished my shopping I walked back to the quay, and as I walked an ambulance sped past me with urgent clamour. There is a little pub halfway along the quay, and a woman came out of the doorway to stop me.

"I was asked to keep a look out for you," she said. "There's been an accident at the ship, but the skipper wasn't injured. I was to be sure to tell you that."

I thanked her and hurried along the quay. Outside the agent's office my skipper was waiting to stop me going any further. It was a great relief to see him, because you know when somebody tells you that everything is "all right" you don't instinctively believe them. We went back inside the broker's office where they told me that the crane had overbalanced and the jib had collapsed right across the *Olive May's* forehold. The man who helped to load by signalling the crane driver when to open the grab, had been standing directly beneath the jib. He was killed instantly. We were all friendly with this man, so of course it was a shock and I was terribly upset. The broker was very kind to me and drove me straight away to his home in the nearby countryside, where I stayed for the rest of the day with his wife. I recovered later and was taken back to the ship. The hatchway, bow rail and deck were badly damaged, so the scrap which had been in the hold was unloaded again and the ship was taken round to Burnham on Crouch to be repaired, a job that lasted many weeks.

Once again the skipper and I were out of work. He went away to drive heavy lorries for British Road Services; I got a job in a market garden, pinching out shoots on young tomato plants (if the weather was dry) or carnations in greenhouses (if wet). Then my skipper decided to buy the *Dingle* — a deal done by correspondence with the owner in the far west of Ireland. When it was all settled, off we went to collect her and bring her back to England.

Chapter Eight

Tales of Irish Mice

THE *Dingle*'s new crew comprised the former skipper and mate of the *Olive May* and an old codger called Harry who had made a series of trips with us and had been found very useful on board, being an ex-Royal Navy man, very handy with carpentry and engines. He must have been in his seventies, though spry and irritatingly cheerful at all times. The three of us travelled by a late train from Euston to Holyhead with Irishmen drinking Guinness, and crossed to Dun Laoghaire on what must have been (I presume) the worst passage of the year, taking exactly twice the scheduled time for crossing in the teeth of a westerly gale. Although not quite sick, I knew I daren't set foot in the reeking passenger accommodation (we were far too poor to afford private cabins), so I spent the six hour voyage standing at a rail on a sort of veranda abaft the passenger saloon. What misery was around me! People similarly avoiding the revolting saloon, trying to keep their balance on widespread feet while the ship rolled beneath them; the roaring of the gale; icy salt spray. Further aft from the place where I was standing where the forward bulkhead of the crew's accommodation started there was a young man crouched in a sheltering angle of the deck; rolled tightly into a ball, feet and head tucked out of sight, he remained in that position for hours until we reached harbour. The skipper, who didn't like the cold, eventually came out of the saloon and joined me at the rail, saying that the heat and vomit had become too much even for his hard stomach. Daylight crept upon us. I stirred from my position to take a peek around the corner into the wind and was relieved to see that land was in sight. The ship was now getting some shelter from the proximity of the land and was much steadier. The passengers were emerging from their state of nausea and numbness and thankfully preparing to disembark.

We took the train from Dublin to Limerick and then the bus to a small port near the mouth of the Shannon, where we found our new ship the *Dingle*. We stayed there two weeks getting her into a fit state for the voyage back to Essex. She had not ventured beyond the Shannon for many years, her trade being the general cargo of that river. The engine had to be surveyed and the skipper instructed in its management; hatches and cloths needed to be put right; wooden plugs must be made for the ventilators in case of bad weather; and the accommodation — oh my! that accommodation! It was in a most deplorable state — a pigsty! A fleapit!! A rats' nest!!! and much worse . . . The crew's quarters aft consisted of a central saloon with a sleeping cabin on each side. In place of a table there was a wide bench set against the forward bulkhead with lockers beneath; on this bench a long leatherette covered cushion. I was down there shortly after our arrival and suddenly the cushion *rippled* from the inside. After recovering from my surprise I saw that it had mice in it. Mice? — they were everywhere — in the bunks, cushions and lockers; they ran along the frames between the hold and cabin; there were colonies of them in the fo'c'sle which (although fitted with a bunk) was filled with ship's stores, wire, rope, anchor chain, buckets and a stock of peat.

There was a large free-standing stove in the middle of the saloon with a chimney which led up through the deck. The fuel used was peat and the floor of the cabin around the stove was quite three inches deep in peat dust, compressed hard by passing feet. (This we broke up and shovelled into sacks for later burning, and eventually we uncovered a linoleum flooring.)

The *Dingle* had lain afloat for years, never taking the ground and always using deep water berths. Her bilges were bone dry throughout the length of the ship — perhaps I should say dust dry, because they were completely stuffed up with wheat which had slipped through small gaps in the ceiling (in a ship the floor of the hold is known as the ceiling — alternative spelling, sealing). If she had ever sprung a leak, none of the pumps, hand or mechanical, would have been of any use; they would instantly have choked on the wheat from the bilges. So the hundreds of Irish mice who had built a city of nests would be quite safe until the ship got round to Essex, but more of them later.

The mouse-ridden and (as I discovered to my alarm) flea-ridden cushions were hoisted on deck and thrown on to the quay where a great pile of rubbish from the ship was accumulating. I returned from the town one day after an errand to buy two pounds of nails (for long after referred to as "those bloody useless Irish nails") to find an old lady standing near a pile of rubbish. She said something to me, but in Erse, and all I could do was give a friendly smile and shrug my shoulders — whereupon she changed to a heavily accented English: "Would you be throwing those things away? Not wanted then?" Very doubtfully I replied, yes, but they wouldn't be of any use to her, they were very dirty. She muttered something that sounded like ". . . do well enough for the childer" and then hoisted one of the locker cushions on to her back and staggered off up the quay. Soon everything we put on the dump had disappeared.

To supplement the supply on board we ordered a load of peat from the town; this arrived on the quay one day in a small cart pulled by a diminutive donkey. The donkey driver lifted the peats one at a time from the cart and threw them to me as I stood on the foredeck and I tossed them down into the fo'c'sle where Harry was waiting to stow them. "Three hundred and thirty-three," Harry announced when he had finished the stowing; he'd been keeping a tally. Fifteen shillings I think they cost and they lasted us the whole trip round and then some over which was burnt while on the shipyard at Wivenhoe. It was September and already the nights were chilly; the stove was also the only source of heat for cooking. Glowing hot and with a pleasant aroma of peat and the kettle singing on the top, the stove would make a pleasant place to come down to when off watch.

Eventually we got the ship into some sort of order. The engine was pronounced fit, but we required bunkers; a load of gas oil was delivered by road tanker. An extremely officious and bustling representative of the Irish Board of Trade made himself known to us and after inspecting the ship made out a list as long as your arm of work required to be done before we could be allowed clear of Irish waters. We managed to satisfy his requirements on the small jobs and as regards the lifesaving equipment (which had been sent over from England); but the skipper told him that there were no facilities here for the larger work and could we motor round to Cork to get it done? This he agreed to, and actually stood on the quay the day we left, and the last thing he said to us was: "See you in Cork, Skipper." The skipper echoed: "Yes, see you in Cork!" (having not the least intention of being found in Cork, not if *he* could help it).

We left Kilrush with six on board. These were the skipper and mate, Harry, two Irishmen who were the *Dingle*'s crew before we bought her, and a sort of pilot to see us clear a little way beyond Slattery Island, whose motor boat we towed astern. I think it was around two in the afternoon when we set off, a beautiful day, no wind, and the sort of hazy sunshine that makes the sky and smooth water all one silvery pearl

colour. We had the right charts on board, and the skipper and old
Harry laid off courses to take us southwards from a point off Loop Head
to the Blasket Islands, a distance of some forty miles.

Either they underestimated the speed of the *Dingle* in the ideal
conditions of that day or we had an extremely favourable tide roaring
along with us; it seemed no time at all after leaving Loop Head astern
that I looked out and cried: "That's an island, isn't it? But it can't be!
It's far too early!" But soon we were threading our way through a maze
of jagged black rocks and crossing the wide entance of Dingle Bay.
Ahead of us lay the island of Valencia, and as it was growing dusk the
skipper decided we might as well spend the night there. On the other
side of the island was the quietest, safest anchorage one could wish for.
Green land swept smoothly up and away on all sides; there wasn't
another ship or boat to be seen, nor people, nor even any sheep; only a
few gulls and utter peace. I cooked an evening meal and we weren't
late turning in. There were no mattresses on the bunks (we'd thrown
them all ashore, hadn't we); only a few blankets that we had brought
with us and lifejackets for pillows. My night was so disturbed by mice
running over me upon their unlawful occasions, that it was a relief
when the time came to get up, and listen to the early shipping forecast,
which was a good one. Then up anchor and on our way once again —
across the Kenmare entrance, through Bantry Bay (where my father's
Royal Navy ship went early in the Great War for gunnery practice) on
to pass between Cape Clear and Fastnet Rock, and some twelve hours
out of Valencia to round Old Head of Kinsale into another safe
anchorage, Kinsale Harbour. From there, of course, we were expected
to continue up to Cork and have those expensive adjustments made to
the ship which the Irish Board of Trade demanded. Instead, next
morning, after hearing another favourable forecast, we set off at dawn
in a dead straight line for Lands End — and the devil take the Irish
Board of Trade!

It was a splendid run. We passed the Wolf in the middle of the
night, and the following day, after hearing an adverse weather
forecast, we went into Brixham Harbour where we lay out a southerly
gale for a couple of days. It was there that the skipper ordered me
ashore to buy a saw. I didn't know anything about saws; evidently he
wanted me to procure a plain, simple, everyday saw, costing about
seven and six, but in the shop my fancy was taken by a queen of the
species, a Spear and Jackson at twenty-five bob. *"How much?"* the
skipper exclaimed when I got back with it. Really, though, it was an

extremely good buy, for that saw lasted years and years, doing a prodigious amount of work. As I have said, my skipper did all his own carpentry on board, the heaviest task being when worn boards of the ceiling needed to be replaced — planks three inches thick, ten or twelve inches wide and impregnated with sand. The saw even survived my usage, and I'm a wretched sawyer.

When the gale had moderated, we came out of Brixham and bowled away up Channel — one night behind the Isle of Wight, then non-stop to the Colne without incident. A couple of days later the *Dingle* was positioned on the cradle at Wivenhoe shipyard, and drawn up the slipway into the shed where we would remain several weeks.

We took up all the ceiling boards to clean and paint the bilges. The shipyard men had a great time chasing our mice and such rats as then appeared. We set a dozen baited traps in the cabin and when I was alone of an evening painting out the accommodation, my attention to the accompanying radio music was often interrupted by: "Snap, squeak", when I would put down my paint brush, pick up the appropriate trap and its victim, and dispose of the corpse over the side, resetting the trap and then resuming painting. Any squeamishness I may originally have felt was quickly overcome by the urgent need to rid the ship of its unwanted guests. At length the supply of mice dried up; suddenly there were no more. The last of the vermin that came to light was a rat which was enthusiastically chased by a couple of shipwrights and despatched with a chipping hammer.

Many changes were made to the structure of the ship. The heavy mast situated between the main and foreholds was removed and the hold shortened from aft for a one hatchway layout. A new system of beams across the hold to take the hatches was designed and fabricated; the outer bulwarks were cut away for the length of the hold and replaced by stanchion and wire safety rails. The hull and bottom and frames and stringers were completely cleaned of rust, thoroughly wire brushed, undercoated and finally painted. Both the skipper and I worked alongside the yard men making use of the yard's tools and power. The amount of chipping that can be done with an air powered chipping hammer, as compared with a manual hammer, is phenomenal. Of course, like most mechanical tools, it had its disadvantages: the amount of noise and flying dust and rust chips were in direct proportion to the greater speed and no-one at that yard then seemed to have heard of eye or ear protection. Because of the impressive area of clean metal resulting from an hour or so of work with an air hammer I greatly enjoyed doing it. I did a lot of this work on the inside bottom and on two occasions found a thin spot where the hammer went right through — once when the tide was up around us and a pretty fountain of water resulted! I had to copy the Dutch boy, while screaming for help!

The extra room added to the aft accommodation from the shortening of the hold was made into a galley/washroom and — what elegance! — a marine toilet. To replace the large mast we had a much smaller one made, the regulation height to take the masthead light and with it a counterweight at the bottom so that I could easily lower and raise it singlehanded when going through the Thames bridges. We did a lot of work up to Wandsworth and I became a dab hand at lowering the mast just sufficient to get through the lowest of the bridges (was it Waterloo?) without wasting an inch of space. The skipper had warned me that if I as much as touched any one of the bridges, I would be required to buy a complete new bridge!

We were many weeks on the shipyard getting all this work done; we were fully occupied outside throughout the hours of daylight, then with the yard's electric lights on long leads down in the accommodation in the evenings and it seemed as if the turmoil and mess would go on indefinitely. But eventually we were ready to start trading, and on a medium spring tide we were relaunched with a most satisfying swoosh down the slipway.

Chapter Nine

The Sand Work

THERE is an arm of the merchant navy known in the trade as "sandies" or "ballastmen". As yet unhonoured and unsung, (though not unvocal as the continuous conversation on the shipping frequency will testify), their vessels are usually purpose built and carry two to three hundred tons of sand, gravel and ballast, in the various proportions required to make the concrete so necessary in present times for all kinds of construction work.

They usually have one big hold for speedy loading and discharge and a crew of two, sometimes three. They plough back and forth between London and Kentish ports and the various ballast pits of Essex which have access to rivers or creeks. The loading berths are tidal. Except on spring tides they are much restricted in depth, often with less than ten feet available to float a loaded barge off the berth at high water. So most of the sandies have a loading draft of about seven feet which is why they are many and small: many fewer vessels of a greater capacity would be a lot more economical to run, but in the geographical circumstances simply not feasible. Unlike general cargo barges, which can often find a freight in both directions, the sandies always make the return trip to Essex unladen. They demand a quick turn round at both ends of the voyage, and can load or unload on every high water, at roughly twelve hour intervals. The empty barge arrives at the loading berth on the flood tide as soon as there is enough water alongside and is loaded by crane and grab from nearby heaps, or else from an overhead conveyor belt which carries the material to the wharf from further inland. One of the crew keeps an eye on the loading, making sure the final trim of the vessel is even, and as soon as loading is complete, if it's close to high tide, they motor off into deeper water to cover the hold with hatches and tarpaulins. If there happens to be time in hand, and no other barge is waiting to take the berth, they cover the hold before leaving, and perhaps have a meal and listen for the gale warnings on the radio. Then, just before high water, down the river they go, out into the North Sea and up the Swin to London, perhaps to Rochester or Sheerness in the Medway; worst of all (from the point of view of access) Hoo, or Sittingbourne. The Essexmen used to reckon taking a freight anywhere in Kent was going foreign!

The ballast trade is carried on night and day, summer and winter. A barge will arrive at a berth in London at, perhaps, two in the morning, and the crew will turn in after uncovering the hatchway (though this job has sometimes already been done by the mate while still under way in the Thames to save loss of sleep time) — only to be relentlessly awakened at 6 a.m. by the roar of the crane and the crash of the grab in the hold. The skipper will go on shore during the morning to transact certain business at the wharf office and pick up orders for the next job; the mate will wander off to the nearest shop to buy a small amount of provisions for the next round trip — there is rarely time at the loading end to be spared for domestic matters. If there's a workman's café or a pub close by the crew may decide to have a bite ashore. Then, sometime around high water, off they go again, not bothering to replace the hatches unless the weather is expected to be extremely rough outside the river — to arrive at their loading berth back in Essex by the following half flood.

How easy it all sounds in that short paragraph! Perhaps it is easy when most of the crews are employed men, working for established companies with proper offices ashore. They put in the hours, get their pay for the number of freights they carry, and if they manage to survive the cruel sea, the fog and gales and ice, and encountering fishermen without lights, and gigantic ships travelling at twenty knots on radar, and engine breakdown in awkward places, and sudden leaks and running out of grub when forced to lay fogbound or windbound miles from any shops, mates who go home for Sunday and fail to turn up at midnight sailing (thus losing the tide and incurring the wrath of the Office manager) — if they can survive all that (and more) then they'll probably live to draw their pensions and grow leeks for show.

The *Dingle,* as well as coping with all contingencies and predicaments had the extra dimension that she was skipper-owned. There was no office ashore, and the skipper had to go to the big companies seeking contracts, working out the least cost per cubic yard carried at which his vessel could make a living and some small profit, and still induce the companies to use his services. The calculation of price per cubic yard is complicated by various materials differing in weight. In the *Dingle* we were unable to carry as many cubic yards of ballast as we could of sand or small gravel, so the price for carrying ballast had to be higher than that for gravel. Also, we could carry material from Essex to Medway ports more cheaply than right up to London, running expenses being less for the shorter passage, although the number of freights achieved weekly was about the same.

If the building trade had a quiet spell we might get alternative freights of general cargo such as sawn timber, or whole logs from London to the small ports of Essex or Kent. But the *Dingle* was much restricted in her carrying capacity (and thus in earning power) because she had been converted from a general cargo carrier specifically to work in the ballast trade. (Nor had cargo work been her original purpose when built: enthusiasts will find at the end of the book a note about this and other First World War landing craft constructed for the Dardanelles campaign which subsequently were to earn their living for a further fifty years trading around the coast.) For this new work, she was structurally altered from having one large and one small hold (with a lot of space under the decks), to a single hold which was in fact immediately under the lengthened hatchway, that part which was under the side decks being boarded off so when unloading the grab could pick up most of the ballast without the need of a trimmer to shovel it from inaccessible nooks towards the middle.

A skipper-owner would usually maintain and manage his craft more carefully — in the sense that he would exercise greater caution in attempting the Swin in bad weather when damage to the hull might result from a battering by the sea. Because the *Dingle* had a spoon shaped bow, she was particularly vulnerable when running down empty against an easterly swell. A sailing barge has a straight stem and the bottom is flat from rudder post to stem except for her fore and after runs; but the *Dingle* had a very short stem from which the bottom sloped away at an angle until it met the keel some ten feet aft. When under way without cargo, and at normal full ahead revs, this shape caused the barge to plane and thus increase her speed through the water. Planing lifted the first ten feet clear of the water, but when heading into an easterly swell, this swim section slammed with terrific force on the waves, throwing spray high in the air. It was an interesting experience. Sometimes the hammering would stop her dead in her tracks and it would take many seconds before she could pick up speed and resume her planing. The danger in this was that such hammering could easily loosen rivets or even force a plate inwards; and though this might not be noticed at the time, when loaded the damaged place would be deep in the water and under pressure, causing flooding such as the pumps might not be able to cope with. Sometimes the material we had to load arrived in the hold saturated with rain water which eventually seeped down into the bilges, so that I often came up on deck with the report: "Water's over the cabin floor, but I've had a taste and its fresh,"; and the skipper would have to start the pump that emptied the bilges. So it will not surprise the reader to learn that we didn't have a Persian rug laid on the cabin floor. Any damage caused by knocking up the bottom plates would necessitate repair work which could only be done on a shipyard; such expense, and the loss of earnings which resulted was always something to be avoided. Thus, if the winds were from anywhere east and we were bound down Swin, by the time we were abeam of Southend a critical decision needed to be made: would it be wise to attempt the passage, or should we instead go over into Sheerness until the seas moderated? Sometimes we would venture outside, only to repent and turn back into Sheerness. On such occasions we might leave other barges of identical build to continue down Swin, pounding into the swells with spray and spume flying — which was depressing for us for we knew that we, too, *could* get down, but must not risk incurring expensive damage.

Nowadays, because of radar, I suppose there aren't many occasions when dense fog stops all shipping in the Thames Estuary, but thirty years ago, the regular occurrence, throughout the year, of fog, was a constant nuisance and worry to the little ships of the ballast trade. Setting out from the middle reaches of the Colne, we would cautiously feel our way by compass and echo sounder from buoy to buoy down to Colne Point, and then out past the Eagle to the Knoll, down to the Spitway buoy south of Clacton, which had a nice loud bell on it through that narrow tideswept gutway (echo sounder specially useful here), and up Swin along the western edge of the channel. Of course, we had the help of these few navigational aids, but even so every ship has its own idiosyncrasies when laying off a course on a chart, and so during the many fine runs up and down in clear daylight we compiled an exercise book of the exact courses by compass, and precise timings, from buoy to buoy in both directions — in light and loaded trim — all the way from Gravesend to Brightlingsea, up the Blackwater to Osea Island, and in the Crouch as far as Burnham. So, under way in thick weather we went literally by the book. When, according to the clock, the next buoy was calculated to be close, it was my job to go up forward and keep a lookout for it. According to our position in relation to the buoy the skipper would make his adjustment, then resume steering by the book. If, when the requisite time had elapsed, we had failed to find the buoy, we would nevertheless alter our course as the book required and start a new timing. The fact that the system unerringly worked never failed to amaze and delight me. I wonder if those who navigate the vast oceans can feel any greater satisfaction than mine when their complex mathematics eventually bring them to a successful landfall! In our work with the hazard of sandbanks close on either hand, there was all too little margin for error.

If the fog was still thick by the time we made our way up as far as the Blacktail buoy (not far from Shoeburyness and the resort of Southend on Sea once so popular with London holidaymakers) we would sneak over into the least possible depth of water, drop our anchor and wait for an improvement before venturing into the crowded Thames tide. We would stand our beautiful brass bell on the hatchway and occasionally one or the other of us would go on deck and give it a vigorous ten-second shake to inform the invisible world of our presence. There was little fear from big ships; they would remain in the deep water; but plenty of other barges like us, as well as small coasters, could be expected to be in our vicinity.

Every sound came clearly to us even down below in the cabin. The slap of little waves along our sides, occasionally the splash on the nearby sand of the wash from some intrepid ship under way with radar; the desolate mew of seagulls; bells ringing out in the channel where bigger ships were anchored (some of them, instead of ringing bells, appeared to clash spoons on frying pans!). One sound that would always bring the crew leaping up on deck was that of human voices. Maybe a solitary cockle boat, feeling its way back to Leigh would pass in close, dimly seen, with a figure hunched against the damp cold on the stemhead keeping a look out. Sometimes it would be another barge on passage, touching alongside for a chat (though the swells made it uncomfortable for two barges to lie together), before dropping away a short distance to let go their own anchor.

There was one period of fog to be long remembered by those of us caught out in it. It was nearly Christmas and we came out of Colne in company with several other craft on a Tuesday afternoon, got up as far as the Blacktail and lay at anchor there until the Thursday afternoon, by which time some were in a serious state of hunger. We were all right, because we kept an ample store cupboard. I hate wasting food, but usually overstocked with bread and other basic perishables and always kept a good store of tinned food. Many of the barges maintained a less prudent economy; hoping always to be in London every other tide they catered strictly on a daily basis.

There was much wailing on the shipping frequency. The shortage of cigarettes caused most sorrow. My skipper was an inveterate pipe smoker. Usually he was careful to keep a sufficient stock of tobacco on board. But by this Thursday morning even he was scraping the last few shreds from the bottom of the tin. But relief from that particular misery was close at hand: I had bought a two ounce tin of his favourite brand for a Christmas present and mightily appreciative he was when I produced it! Eventually we heard on the radio that up at Gravesend the fog was starting to lift with the coming of a westerly land breeze and we all prepared to get our anchors as soon as it looked safe. The breeze reached us and visibility cleared like magic. What a sight the Estuary presented at that moment! A veritable armada; ships of every size, shape, colour and nationality — from supertankers down to fishermen, all bound up the Thames or into the Medway. There must have been a great shortage of pilots that day. We were bound upalong so could maintain our course on the right hand side of the channel but it must have been hair-raising for any vessel who was a bit slow in crossing the Estuary athwart all the inward bound traffic.

Chapter Ten

Icebound up the Creek

THE sand and ballast quays in the Essex rivers are situated in awkward, hazardous and unreasonable places. There is not a lot to choose between them for dreadfulness, though each one is utterly different from the next. The little broken jetty at Fingringhoe in my day poked out like a finger into the tideway so that on approaching the upper berth on the flood the tide tried to carry us away up the river while the mate desperately fought to get a turn round a post to enable the skipper to manoeuvre alongside; if we were required to load on the down river side the tide slammed us against the piles, so we lay pinned like a butterfly and full force of the engine had to be used to shift along to a position under the chute. If we had to lie over two high waters, the retreating tide tried to drag the barge from the pier; if we should have to remain there aground, awaiting better tides, it was miles and miles to the nearest shop and pub. But it was a pleasant enough situation in which to be beneaped. Blackberries were to be had for the picking in season, and half a dozen nightingales vied for supremacy in the rough shrubland around the pits, all night long (well, yes you can have too much of a good thing!).

When it was necessary to go up in the dark to load at Martins Farm (a comparatively new jetty then), a mile or so up Brightlingsea Creek, our course was fraught with the danger of mowing down a multitude of yachts and fishing boats, with not a light among them, all lying about the fairway.

Worst of all, though, was the berth up Alresford Creek, an arm of the Colne just a mile or so above Brightlingsea. Other barges preferred not to go there. I reckon in our day we were doing most of the Alresford work. The mouth of the creek was wide, but the channel itself very narrow and winding, without the benefit of buoys or even withies to show the way. Entry was barred by a railway bridge with a swing section. This needed to be opened manually by two railmen to leave a gap of one and a half barge widths. There were no lights of any kind and I seem to remember we mostly went through on dark tides. The men, who came from the nearest railway station to open it, had a hand torch with which to signal to us that the bridge was open; we couldn't see whether it was open or not. They were always extremely anxious lest we should damage the bridge machinery as we went through; unless they could get the bridge closed behind us, they were trapped on an island! The pit office would telephone the railway station staff some hours before we were due to request the bridge to be opened.

We usually arrived off the mouth of the creek as soon as there was water and hovered as close as we could safely get, trying to make out if there was any kind of activity in the bridge area. Sometimes I spotted a small wavering light as the men walked along the bridge from the land swinging a torch. If very calm, we could hear their voices. When we thought the men were signalling to us that the bridge was open, the skipper steered towards the still invisible gap, while I stood forward with a searchlight on a long lead and shouted back any change of heading I thought necessary. The course of the channel required a barge to approach on a heading of south-east; as soon as the bow was in the opening, the heading had to become north-east to get through; as soon as the stern was clear through the bridge, a south-easterly heading was resumed. These fine, rapid adjustments could only be achieved in ideal conditions: calm and clear. If it was foggy the whole operation was carried out like a game of blind man's buff, the only guide being the men's voices; it was Russian roulette whether we hit the gap or the piles or the bridge! If it was clear and windy we often went through crabwise, trying desperately to avoid clouting the swing portion of the bridge with our bow (which was high) and at the same time to avoid catching one of the stone pillars with our quarter (which was low on the water). If it was raining heavily, neither the skipper nor I could see much of anything at all as we both wore glasses! I reckon we more often touched than missed. There would be furious shouts from the men on the bridge (who appeared to think we did it to annoy), but we were away up the creek and tying up at the degenerate ruins of the ballast wharf ready for loading next morning. I suppose the bridgemen could have come chasing angrily after us when they had shut the bridge, but they never did; better to get off home to bed I suppose. I bet there was a black book at the station, recording clashes between barge and bridge, though Lord knows we did try most faithfully on every occasion to avoid it.

It was at this wharf that we lay ten days during the January of that bad winter of 1962/3. There were ice floes in the Colne, and we had some hours to wait before we could get in Alresford Creek. We let go our anchor outside and went below to catch up on our lost sleep; but when we turned out again we discovered to our horror that the barge had dragged a mile upstream with the weight of the ice collected around the hull. Later we did manage to get into the creek and on the berth without incident, and lay there ready to load next day, but before we could get away the creek froze up solid right across and though we were loaded, trimmed and covered up, we were unable to move until the thaw came a fortnight later. Three times I trudged up past the quarry to get to the local shop to replenish supplies. The skipper went home knowing the barge was safe where she lay and that nothing could be done till the thaw. There were always plenty of books on board and I had a radio. I usually had some knitting or sewing to do, for I made most of my own clothes. Seeing the birds in dire straits I used to scatter a bit of bread about, though usually it was taken by the pigeons, those great survivors; smaller birds had vanished and the ducks on the ice were dead.

On reflection, though, perhaps loading ballast at what was known as Westie's Beach was even more awkward for a barge than getting into Alresford Creek. The few occasions when we loaded there were before the days of the *Dingle,* while we were still working for Samuel West from whom the place took its name. The beach lies along the eastern edge of the Colne Estuary, just below Brightlingsea. There was neither wharf nor pier. The barges merely came and sat on the beach shortly after high water, hopefully grounding in the required place, to be loaded by a mobile tracked crane. The crane driver worked only during daylight so the operation of getting on and off the beach was usually performed in darkness. The crane driver would plant a stake in position the previous low water, and the barge was required to come at precisely the correct state of tide, find this stake, and try to take the ground parallel to the beach so that the stake was alongside the middle of the hold. But it's an imperfect world, and if it was windy our placing rarely satisfied these stringent requirements. Sometimes in fog, we failed to find the stake at all, and just lay on the beach haphazardly, hoping we were somewhere near the appointed spot.

The prevailing wind blew straight on to the shore and the barge was likely to get knocked further up than was required, which meant she couldn't take a full load and still be able to float off at high water. An approach from downstream on the ebb tide found me up forward peering into the gloom — trying to pick out the silhouette of the crane against the skyline on top of the sea wall, out of reach of the tide. Then I would play the searchlight about the surface of the water, seeking the stake, about two feet of which might show stuck up above the surface. If the wind was hard on shore, we'd drop the main anchor as far as possible out into the stream, veer away thirty fathoms of cable, then with a bit of engine shunting (and me pushing on a pole from the starboard quarter) hold the barge in position until she took the ground. The crane driver came along during the morning and grabbed ballast directly from the beach into the hold. There was no way of measuring the amount we loaded, other than by eyeing the pile, and we had to guess at a quantity which would be as great as possible but still allow the barge to float off the beach at high water, and on an even keel, slightly down by the stern rather than by the head — a barge hates to be down by the head and becomes a pig to steer.

If the wind increased, or the forecast for the coming tide was bad, we had to get the crane to push and bully the main anchor further down the beach, and ourselves carry a kedge anchor with a warp from the stern and bury it in the mud at the edge of the water. When the flood came up, and we were near afloat, we'd start the engine, leave it ticking over out of gear, and one of us would wind the main anchor cable on the windlass while the other heaved on the kedge warp to get the barge bodily off the beach. And then everything had to happen at once! The skipper would break out the kedge and haul it aboard, leap into the wheelhouse, put the engine in gear, and I must furiously wind in the last of the chain and break out the anchor, giving a shout to the skipper when it was off the ground. Then, if her stern hadn't swung too close in when she came head to wind, we'd be able to motor away, leaving all on board limp and breathless. We had usually covered up the cargo hold with hatches and cloth and battened down before floating, but leaving one corner open so that I could get below with a shovel and trim out the list if we proved to have one.

Our employers at this time were the London bargeowners, Wests, who once had an extensive sailing fleet, but were now down to a few only, motorised, most of them built of wood. When the skipper and I first went to work for this firm, before our acquisition of the *Dingle*, we took charge of the smaller barges as relief crew for a few weeks at a time until permanent crews came to take over. Although these barges were not built for the sand and ballast work but for general cargo, when we took them over they were mainly employed between the Colne Beach and London, for at that time the trade was prosperous. As well as working off the beach, we also loaded an occasional freight at the wharves at Rowhedge, Fingringhoe and Brightlingsea.

One Christmas time, we tied up the barge on the buoys just below Wivenhoe. The skipper went off home, but I decided to stay overnight and go home the following day, Christmas Eve. In the morning there was a gale of wind blowing straight down the river, and I knew I was not strong enough to scull the small boat up wind and up tide to Wivenhoe, so I resigned myself to staying aboard until it moderated. All that morning the wind continued to blow. After a sparse lunch, I was sitting in the cabin with the radio on when I heard a faint voice calling: "Rescue! Rescue!" I rushed up on deck and there was the skipper coming down in a small boat he'd borrowed from the shipyard. At home he had realised I wouldn't be able to get away and he'd come all the way back to help me get ashore. He was somewhat disgruntled, though, because on the way down river his hat had blown away and was lost forever on the mudflats!

It was while we had this same barge away that he played a diabolical trick on me. We had loaded at Brightlingsea during the day, and had eaten lunch ashore at a local café; for our light evening meal I had bought half a pound of smoked sprats, the delights of which we had recently discovered, and four chocolate eclairs. We loaded and covered up, and leaving on the afternoon high water set out for Rochester. Halfway up the Swin, at about six o'clock (meals were usually timed to coincide with the radio weather forecast), I prepared our tea; buttered slices of brown bread, the sprats divided with scrupulous fairness between two plates and the eclairs arrayed on another; tea brewing under the cosy. Then I went up to relieve the skipper at the wheel. (Skippers, by long tradition, always eat first, then mates.) I hadn't earlier let on what we were going to have for our tea, and when my captain returned to the wheelhouse, half an hour later, carrying his second mug of tea, he condescended to comment favourably on the meal. I went below for my tea. But — O malheur! the table was bare! Not so much as a sprat's head to be seen! Not a single eclair within miles; only empty plates on the table! Back I went up top.

"Did you eat *all* the sprats?" I cried with indignation.

"Why, weren't they all for me, then?" the skipper replied with child-like innocence.

I gave a deep, patient sigh and turned to go. Then the man

Grand Coronation Sailing Barge Match, River Thames, 1953.

(22) The *Clara* (above) would have been last in her class, had not the *Glenmore* (below, No 23) broken her topmast after this photograph was taken. The light airs of that morning developed later in the day into the sort of weather that can take the topmast out of a barge if the crew is not quick enough to drop down the staysail.

(24) Coronation race: Spectators on the *Royal Sovereign* and following craft have a fine view of competitors in the restricted staysail class, neck and neck in the early part of the day. (*Esther* and *Revival.*)

(25) Greyhounds of the fleet were the champion bowsprit class barges. The expenditure of large sums of money had brought them to the peak of perfection. On this day it was the *Sara*'s race; her only serious rival, *Sirdar*, was far behind.

(26)   Coronation race: Eastwoods, the brick makers, bought the *Nelson* specially for this match; she did no good.

(27)   The fleetfooted old *Westmoreland* didn't merely carry advertising in her sails: she earned her living carrying bricks in her hold.

(28)   The *Olive May* as I never knew her. This was the day of her launch in 1920. She was built as a fully-rigged sailing barge with auxiliary power.

(29)   By the time I knew her, 35 years later, she relied wholly on her not very reliable Crossley oil engine. Here, while dried out, she is given a coat of tar. We carried a lot of the beach to London in the *Olive May*'s hold.

Above:
(30) *Olive May,* loading china clay at Par, Cornwall.

Left:
(31) At King's Lynn, 1955.

Top: (32)   Up and planing! The *Dingle*'s spoon-bow was an advantage in calm conditions, but *horrible* in any amount of sea.

Above: (33)   Hazardous loading: our agba logs on the *Dingle,* awaiting a calm.

Below: (34)   Having loaded 'a-dry', in re-floating this ballast barge finds she has a severe list to starboard. At a later date the *Helen of Troy* was lost in the Swin.

(35) The motor barge *Lord Roberts* looks deep in her marks in this picture, but she looked even deeper that day in the Whitaker when I went salvaging with my motor pump!

(36) The end of the passage. A rare moment to relax in the sun. . . .

relented. "It's all right, I hid them in the oven!" I had fallen completely for a very old prank, but my relish for those sprats remained unimpaired.

Chapter Eleven

Girl Overboard!

LIKE motor cars, ships with engines require fuelling facilities when their tanks run low. But unlike the roads, where petrol stations are to be found at almost every intersection, sometimes on all four corners (except when a motorist is in dire need), the seaways of the world seem to lack enterprise, and as a rule only the large oil refineries, situated on coast and river, provide facilities for bunkering. The most expensive method of getting fuel to a ship, and one much deplored by owners, is to order up a road tanker to the quayside. It is kinder, by far, to call at bunkering jetties such as are to be found at Purfleet, on the Thames, and at the Isle of Grain at the mouth of the Medway. In the *Dingle* usually we called alongside at Purfleet, after discharging anywhere up the London river. Being the smallest size of ship to visit them, we didn't need to telephone to give advance warning, but rounded to, head in the tide, and went alongside whichever berth happened to be vacant. These jetties are very tall indeed. They cater for ships of ten thousand tons and more; we never put ropes up on the bollards, but instead caught a turn round the wooden piles forward and aft at our own level. The hosepipe, with a great brass nozzle, controlled by a stiff wheel valve at the business end, was lowered by means of a derrick, but before that happened I needed to shout out to the man on the jetty that we would have to have his very smallest nozzle, to fit into our deck filler pipe. The capacity of the tank below was only 500 gallons and some measure of finesse was needed to regulate the flow into the tank so that it didn't spurt out on to the deck. The skipper, who remained in the engine room watching the gauge on the tank, would eventually bellow: *"Right!"*, and I must then spin the handwheel which shut the valve before the fuel overflowed and covered everything for yards around (including me). My success in this was no more than fifty/fifty. When bunkering large ships the man in charge on the jetty needed to operate valves at his own level and meter out tons of fuel; but he reckoned he could fulfil our modest needs with the quantity which happened to be lying in the pipe between the pumphouse and the nozzle.

When we had finished bunkering, the skipper would climb the perilously slippery iron ladder which led to the office to sign the docket, while I swilled a few buckets of river water around the decks to wash away the spillage. As soon as he was back on board I would retrieve the ropes from around the piles, and we'd push off into the tide, wheel hard over to port, and continue our passage down river. The time taken over this operation was usually half an hour, never more than an hour.

But there was one occasion when our stop for bunkers lasted more than a week. We were on our way down from Blackfriars having unloaded sand, and we rounded to as usual in front of the bunkering jetty. As we straightened up after the turn, there was a funny sort of noise — actually perhaps an absence of noise, because the engine sounded as if it was racing out of gear. I was standing up forward ready to get a turn with a rope, when the skipper shouted to me: "Something's up!" I ran back aft; he said in a hollow voice: "I reckon we've lost the prop." I looked over the stern, and sure enough, although the engine was in gear ahead, there was no turbulence to indicate a turning propeller. Fortunately the ebb tide was tending to set us against the jetty, so we didn't have to drop the anchor in the middle of the fairway; we were able to ease alongside, and I took a quick turn round a pile. It was an awkward situation in which to find ourselves. The skipper went up on the jetty to use the telephone, the outcome of which was the arrival of a small tug to tow us up the river to a shipyard on the Rands where we lay until a new propeller could be delivered and fitted.

While waiting, we did some painting around the ship and general small maintenance work. Also, it was suggested that a diver might be tried to see if our lost propeller could be located on the river bed. So one day a scuba diver came up from Rochester and we took the small boat and outboard engine down to the place in Long Reach where we thought it might be. We timed the operation for an hour before low water. The diver threw himself backwards over the gunwale of the boat in that abandoned way his sort have, and we shunted slowly back and forth over the spot where he had disappeared. The method of warning that a boat was in attendance upon a diver was to fly a red flag, indicating that all other craft should keep well clear. We didn't have such a flag, but we did have a particularly brilliant red cardigan of mine and tied it by the sleeves to an oar stuck upright in the stern of the boat. It was too heavy to stand out in the light airs of that day, but if we saw anything approaching I waved the oar about to attract notice.

The diver certainly tried hard enough, spending over an hour in the water, coming every few minutes or so to report, but eventually with the gathering flood he said it was quite hopeless; the bottom was deep mud and even at slack water there was so much silt in suspension that he couldn't see more than a couple of yards. We never did find that beautiful, four-bladed, phosphor bronze twenty-two inch propeller; it must lie there yet — if anyone cares to search for it. And my cardigan was never quite the same again.

*   *   *

Once at Whitstable with a freight of sand, we lay alongside the quay in what was known as a sucking-down berth. This is where there is a depth of very fine mud; when the tide recedes a loaded vessel with a flat bottom beds herself snugly into it, and when the new tide comes up she is gripped firmly by the mud and just continues to sit there on the bottom while the tide rises inexorably around her. We lay on this berth waiting to be unloaded (there had been some delay with a broken down crane, and it was our second tide there). Dark, cold, early one evening in winter. Down in the cabin I was thinking about getting the tea ready, but first needed to fetch a bucket of coal for the fire from the store in the fo'c'sle. I climbed the cabin ladder, thrust open the door which had been shut tight against the cold, and let out a squeak of horror! The sucking berth was gripping the ship and the water of the harbour was just lapping against the top of the sill of the cabin door. I fell back into the cabin and exclaimed to the skipper: "There's a foot of water on deck, she must be sucking down!" He put on his wellington boots and went up on deck. It was fortunate that the engineroom door was shut, because, being further aft than the cabin door, the water there was well above the sill. So he had to climb on to the engineroom roof and go in through the skylight. The engine started, the skipper came back through the skylight, crossed into the wheelhouse and put the engine alternately into ahead and astern gear to shock the ship out of the grave she had settled herself into. After several minutes of this shunting, the ship suddenly leapt free and shot up three feet, sending the water on deck cascading in all directions, just like a submarine surfacing! This impressive sight called for a cheer from the large group of spectators lining the quayside.

*   *   *

I only fell overboard once in a potentially difficult situation. We were bringing the *Dingle* up London River one dark rainy night, bound for Blackfriars. Old Harry was away with us on this occasion. It was spring tides, and the river was carrying us along at three knots over and above our own seven. We were certainly racing along that night. Now, it was my habit to start uncovering the hatches after we passed Woolwich, so that by the time we arrived on the berth we could all turn in as soon as the ship was tied up. In this process of uncovering single-handed, I had to knock out the wedges on three sides of the hatchway, leaving the foward end of the cloth fixed, drawing the loose canvas from aft forward until it was clear of the hatchway. Our hold was divided into four sections by beams, the middle (transverse) beam being heavy steel and usually remaining in place during the unloading. The two longitudinal beams were of wood and could be lifted out by two persons and slid to the side of the hold out of the way of the grab. The four divisions of the hold were covered by individual hatches, resting one end on the coaming and the other on the centre beam. The hatches were built of wood, some eight feet long, a foot wide, and a handgrip at either end. There were about sixty hatches covering the hold. After removing the hatchcloth, I could start in the middle of the port side, pick up the middle hatch, flip it over from its resting place on to the top of its neighbour, then quickly slide it along the hatchway, using the coaming as a fulcrum, lower it to the deck foward and aft, go back to the middle and deal similarly with the rest of the quarter, ending up with four separate piles of hatches, two on the forward deck and two aft. When we were all tied up at our berth, the skipper and I would then slide the wooden beams to one side and we were ready for unloading.

We had a guardrail all round the outer edge of the deck, made up of steel stanchions and wire rope, and while very necessary at sea, this greatly hampered our movements when uncovering and was always getting damaged in one way or another. It was constructed to be collapsible; and I always took it down before commencing to uncover the hold.

As I have said, we were surging up river at ten knots and just abreast of Greenwich Hospital. It was midnight. The river was dark. There was a steady drizzle of rain, and no other traffic in the reach. I was wearing a tightly buttoned and belted raincoat (but only shoes, not wellingtons) as I worked with the hatches. I finished the two forward sections and was well down to the starboard quarter, lifting a hatch, flipping it over on to the coaming edge — pushed too hard, met solid resistance, lost my balance, tipped over backwards — splash. Gone in a twinkling. It seemed an awful long time before I broke surface again, coughing and spluttering on the most dreadful tasting water. It was warm, and soupy. (Of course, the most unutterable flotsam is found in the London river.) All quite revolting. When I recovered my breath, treading water, I looked around for the *Dingle,* and saw only her stern light, speeding on up the river already two hundred yards away. Then, to my relief I heard the ship's hooter blaring out into the night a frantic short, short, short, long, long, long; short, short, short — non-stop, and rousing the echoes from the shoreside buildings of Greenwich. It was obvious that the skipper had seen me go. With the tide roaring away under him, he couldn't turn the barge round safely at that point, and would have to continue on up river until he found adequate turning space. As luck would have it, there was no other traffic to get tangled up in the operation; had there been a ship coming out of the lower Surrey Dock entrance, with attendant tugs, wanting all the width of the river, the situation would have been perilous.

Afterwards I learned that while the skipper was occupied in manoeuvring, old Harry (who'd been peacefully asleep in the fo'c'sle, and rudely awakened by the din of the ship's hooter) leapt out of his bunk, didn't wait to put on his spectacles, raced on deck in pyjamas, jumped on the hatchway (the quickest way to get aft), and all too soon discovered that there were no hatches on. He landed in the hold, fortunately on a pile of sand, but soon clambered out again and made his way more circumspectly along the deck to the wheelhouse to be apprised of my desperate situation.

In the meantime I was swimming about, nearer to the north side of the river than to Greenwich; and as the *Dingle* was now out of sight I thought I'd better make for the bank and see if I could get ashore. I had no kind of previous experience so I didn't know how long I'd be able to stay afloat fully clothed. I had tried to get rid of my raincoat, but every time I lowered my hands to undo the belt I sank beneath the surface, so gave up the attempt and struck out encumbered as I was for the bank, which I soon reached — only to find myself at the base of a smooth brick wall at least twelve feet high and topped with spiked iron railings. Quite unscaleable. I next allowed myself to drift up river some way, but the wall seemed to continue to infinity without a break. In the end I gave up, and started swimming back to the middle of the river, hoping to meet the returning barge.

Just as on the shore it's said you can never find a policeman when you need one, it's the same in the river, apparently. There are quite a number of those neat little police launches patrolling the river night and day (and when, many *many* years ago, we used to moor alongside a coal lighter, to replenish our stocks for the cabin stove under the cover of darkness, unfailingly their three low navigation lights would be seen by the lookout, sneaking up inside the tiers of moored lighters, close to the sea wall, and we must hastily put away the buckets and be found innocently reading a book in the cabin, whiling away an hour until the tide was right . . .). But on this occasion, despite the audible distress of the *Dingle* in the otherwise quiet night, no police launch put in an appearance. However, other succour was at hand. The *Dingle* had still not returned and I was paddling about like a dog in a pond, being carried by the tide, when down the river, close to the north side out of the worst of the tide, came a little cabin cruiser. I turned towards it and shouted, and was fortunate enough to be heard. They came close to me, and a man and a woman pulled me aboard where I subsided into the cockpit in a sodden heap. I said thank you very much, and here's my barge coming back now to pick me up — if you'd be kind enough to go alongside. The woman produced a beautiful blanket and wanted to swaddle me in it, but I said I wasn't cold and it would only ruin the blanket . . . Then we were alongside the barge and I transferred while we stemmed the tide; away went the little cruiser, the barge turned again as soon as there was room and resumed her interrupted passage up to Blackfriars. We'd lost half an hour, but made our berth with time still to spare. After making fast, the skipper who was feeling anxious, got on the phone to the police station at Wapping with thoughts of typhoid in his mind. "My mate fell overboard at Greenwich, and was safely retrieved, but swallowed a lot of the Thames," he explained. "Is there anything that ought to be done?" The police seemed not to be alarmed; it wasn't necessary to do anything, they said. So we left it at that. I suffered no ill effects, though my stomach must have been a bit cross about it, because for a couple of hours I kept burping, and remembering the appalling taste of London river water.

*   *   *

The building trade is notoriously uncertain. When work fell quiet, the *Dingle* was the first of the sandies to feel it, since normally she did the work that was left after the barge owning companies had fixed their own craft. When this happened we fell back on general carrying — cement from the Medway into Tilbury or London docks to be transferred into big ships for export; timber from London to the Medway and the Essex ports. Economically, the worst we could expect to carry was wheat or beans, because we had a comparatively small hold which, when filled to capacity, did not enable us to carry a decent freight, though it was better than lying idle. Cement was not so bad, being pretty heavy for its bulk, and our perfectly rectangular hold, with no cupboards or wings, was popular with the stevedores and dockers for the great ease of stowage and unloading.

Timber was more difficult. It came aboard as bundles of planks, and in different lengths, widths and thicknesses. My skipper was an old hand at loading timber. In the old days it was a work of art, each plank being stowed separately in the hold to its best advantage, with the aim of leaving as little ullage (unused space) as possible. By the 1950s stevedores seemed to have lost all pride in this sort of achievement and wanted only to get the loading done as quickly as possible, never mind how much or how little the barge went away with. A sling with probably a dozen planks would be suspended above the barge and dropped into the hold where one end would be detached. A sharp tug by the unseen crane, directed by a man on deck, spilled the timber into the hold, where — if the stevedores had their way — it would remain as it fell, an untidy heap. A desultory shift or two while waiting for the arrival of the next sling was all that could be expected from those highly paid slackers. As the skipper and I personally got more money for every additional standard of timber we could carry, we were always busy in the hold when loading. We tried to avoid offending the stevedores, asking politely to borrow a couple of their timber hooks, beautiful tools with smooth wooden handles and shiny points; as soon as the retreating empty sling was clear of the hold, we would energetically set to work, one of us at each end of the pile, to bang hooks into the end of a plank, lift it neatly as far to one side as possible, one after another, to get all the bundle stowed in orderly fashion before the next sling came hovering over the hold.

They reacted to our intrusion in various ways. Sometimes a couple of them would be shamed into applying their efforts in the same direction; some pointedly ignored us and gazed distractedly at the sky; a few were disposed to sneer. But it made no difference to us, for we were determined to get the maximum load of timber aboard. Throughout loading there were long breaks when the stevedores would disappear: breakfast, elevenses, dinner, tea, raining, cold, hot, on strike — there seemed no end to it. While they were gone, leaving their hooks behind, we would further apply ourselves to rectifying the stowage. Don't think, though, that when the load had reached the level of the coamings all loading ceased. On the contrary, having filled the hold, timber was next laid along the decks on either side and piled up and up, until the skipper decided perhaps we'd better say: "Enough". The reason we didn't build the stacks higher than the top of the wheelhouse was that it would have obscured our navigation lights. That effectively stopped us being too greedy!

Several long wires must next be shackled somewhere about the gunwales and carried up the sides of the deck cargo to meet on top in the middle where they were united with bottle screws and made as tight as could be. Hatch cloths were then spread over the stack and roped in place to protect the timber from rain and spray. (Timber absorbs moisture and grows heavier; on a passage of any length that could be dangerous; already the barge was unstable, there being more weight above the deck than below!) With our navigational visibility thus reduced to nothing forward of the wheelhouse, a short ladder needed to be placed at the aft end of the stack for ease of access, and while the skipper stood at the wheel, I would be perched on top of the stack, passing back directions and any news of approaching hazards through the open wheelhouse window. A passage down river was the most awkward. With its relatively narrow reaches and bustling traffic the Thames was no place to be navigating with a blind helmsman, though once below Gravesend it became easier; steering could be done by compass with one or another taking an occasional look around from the top of the stack. How odd we must have seemed — a motorised stack of timber coming down the river, with the mate sitting cross-legged on top, sheltering when it rained under a big black umbrella!

There was one occasion when we had an even more startling load aboard the *Dingle*. We were offered a freight of agba logs from the Tilbury Dock to Maldon. These were great hardwood tree trunks from Africa. They came aboard by crane, one at a time in special rigid spiked lifting frames. They weighed some tons each, and when lowered into the hold the barge sank visibly lower in the water with each one. It didn't take a great many to fill our hold, and a lot of them were too long to fit; but when loading continued above the level of the hatchway we could take much longer trees, stretching from close to the front of the wheelhouse to right up forward. We had no way of securing them, but each one fitted snugly into the hollow between the two beneath, and their weight precluded any fear of shifting. The skipper loaded as many of them as he dared — plus ten more! I should think our centre of gravity must have been half way up the mast. We manoeuvred gingerly out of the Tilbury and down past Gravesend, holding our breaths each time a big ship raced past leaving us to roll in its wake. It was reasonably calm — just a light breeze which we wouldn't have noticed in less hazardous trim; but the skipper decided to put us on the ground close in at Southend to wait until there was an absolutely flat calm and a daylight run. We nosed in on to the shore, to ground about an hour after high water so that we should dry out for most of each tide. We lay for a couple of days in comfort, taking the opportunity first to scrub all round the hull, then apply a coat of black varnish. I have photographs of the barge lying there with her enormous stack of logs, the skipper standing by to give perspective to the scene. The weather continued fine. Eventually we decided it was good enough for the passage down Swin to the Blackwater. Away we went, just before high water, and made our next high tide at Maldon without incident. That must have been a time when both of the crew used one each of their nine lives!

Chapter Twelve

Some Crimes Confessed

"**N**O man would be a sailor who had contrivance enough to get himself into a jail; for being in a ship is being in a jail, with the chance of being drowned . . ." Sam Johnson said it in 1759. I don't know that I go *all* the way with that sentiment. Certainly there have been times at sea when I might have welcomed the comparative warmth, dryness, comfort and easygoing way of life to be found in a modern prison; but the feeling quickly vanishes at the end of the passage, when aching muscles and tired eyes can be relaxed in the indescribable luxury of a barge's cabin. And I have been twice in jail, so perhaps I can speak with some kind of authority.

Way back in the mists of time, I spent a night in a police cell in Zurich, having come to the end of my resources after roaming inconsequentially around France and Switzerland for several weeks. A drop-out before it became the fashion, I had quit my job as a secretary at the BBC (without giving formal notice) and set off to the Continent with no purpose except a vague desire to survey a different scene. Anyway, I terminated my perambulations, foot-sore, unkempt, and hungry at Zurich, spent a day looking round to see if I could get work (fruitlessly), then in the evening surrendered myself to the mercy of the police. They gave me a bed for the night in a cell (but didn't offer to feed me) and the following morning passed me on to the British Consul where I was seen by a minor official who relieved me of my passport and gave me a temporary document in its place, which shamingly identified me as a Distressed British Subject. He bought my ticket at the railway station, and handed me ten francs to sustain me during my ignominious journey home to England. It took me many months to save the sum required and repay His Majesty's Government for their outlay on my behalf, and thus recover my passport.

My other encounter with durance vile was Wormwood Scrubs, ten years later. During the night we had berthed the *Dingle* at Blackfriars, and next morning, while unloading, the manager of the Wharf office

brought the ship some mail, among which was a letter addressed to
me. I opened it with no great interest, then let out an involuntary
squeak of surprise on seeing the place from which it had come! H.M.
Prison, Wormwood Scrubs. The letter was an appeal to me to go and
visit the writer, who mentioned that he'd rather the skipper shouldn't
know. (Too late! The skipper was sitting across the table looking at me
questioningly; I'd been taken by surprise and am never good at a quick
cover up; I had to read it to him.) The letter was from an ex-crew
member of ours, a young man from one of the furthermost corners of
the Commonwealth, who had joined us for a few weeks in the summer.
He'd seen a situations vacant ad which the skipper had placed on a
notice board in a club in London frequented by visitors from abroad.
For a while he sailed about the East Coast with us, then left to go third
hand in another craft plying the same trade. We were occasionally in
touch during the radio chat that went on between the crews of coasting
vessels. He didn't say in his letter why he was in prison, but mentioned
that it was for six months and he would be glad of a visit. He had no
friends or relations in the country.

There was a visiting day once each month, and it was some time
until the next appointed day was due, so I wrote a long, chatty letter
assuring him of my attendance on that day. There followed a further
letter from him accompanied by a stiffly worded note from the Prison
Authorities pointing out that letters to prisoners should be restricted to
two sides of a small sheet of paper. There was a further letter in each
direction — and a warning from our friend that I was not allowed to
crowd so many words into that restricted space! Finally the visiting day
arrived (luckily we were again berthed in London); I stood at the gates
of Wormwood Scrubs and rang a highly polished brass bell. I was
admitted, stated whom I wanted to visit, and was shown into a large
waiting room immediately inside the main gate. The room was filled
with rows of wooden benches occupied mainly by women and children,
and dominated by an enormous coal fire, the flames roaring up the
chimney from a bed of coal as large as could possibly be
accommodated in the old-fashioned hearth. What a blaze! It threw a
warm, cheerful glow over the waiting people and the room buzzed with
chatter. Every now and then someone would come to the door of the
room and shout out a list of names, and off would march a group of
visitors. Then I heard our friend's name, and went out of the waiting
room through the inner yard and into a room which resembled a large
British Rail cafeteria, with its small tables and chairs (but without any

refreshments); there sat our erstwhile third hand. He seemed cheerful and pleased to see me and we chatted of this and that. I had taken him a bag of boiled sweets as a present, through which we crunched our way as we talked. I asked him why he was there, and he told me that he had taken a swing at a policeman who had annoyed him in the Fulham Road one night and had further irritated the magistrate next morning. Six months without the option.

My overwhelming impression of the people I saw in the prison, both prisoners and visitors, was how ordinary — how every-day — how remarkably decent they all looked; not great hulking, glowering evildoers, likely to hit me over the head and relieve me of my scanty purse; not sly, slithery snakes in the grass, ready on the instant to rob any widow and orphan of their savings, pitiless and without remorse. On the contrary, they seemed as innocent and inoffensive as any bunch of people one might observe at random on the streets outside those high walls. Our friend was philosophic about his sentence, and prepared to plod through it without making trouble, and so to gain full remission. He thought he would probably take off for the south of France when released. After my visit we exchanged a few more letters, then he was transferred to an open prison somewhere in Kent to finish his sentence. I heard he became the star of the prison cricket team; after that, nothing more.

I have no desire to further my acquaintance with our penitentiary system. I gave up long ago my own life of crime; nowadays I have the morbid fear of being caught redhanded even in the most trivial misdemeanours — and any infant would be able to see instantly through my lies.

But let me confess to one or two things — just a few of the undetected crimes of my youth which I remember still, though I am assured that time must leave me immune from just retribution.

There was the occasion when we were lying in the South West India Dock waiting to take wheat out of a ship. It was evening, and the wharves were deserted; all the cranes were silent with their jibs neatly stowed in the same direction. We were going ashore for a drink at a nearby pub and on the way to the dock gate came across dozens of oranges, spilled on the ground during unloading. Ever on the lookout for free food I collected as many as I could hold, then looked up to find a dockyard policeman standing a few feet away: "Gulp!" I exclaimed. The policeman looked severely at me and said: "Just don't try taking them outside the dock gate." So I crept sheepishly back on board with my booty before rejoining the skipper, who had disowned me, he not being much interested in such trivial pickings. (He ate his share, I may say, not without enjoyment!)

Another crime I committed very early in my career as a barge mate was when we had the sailing barge *Clara* and were working our way through the congestion of the Surrey Docks to load timber out of a ship the following morning. Throughout the night there were several sailing barges pushing and heaving among the cluster of drifting lighters to reach the ships they were to load from, the crews combining to help one another with the work. It was a clear, silent night and bargemen being what they were (poor, short of food, some commodities still being rationed after the end of the war — and ever ready to take advantage of a benign providence) were considering the possibilities of various lighters, lifting the corners of hatchcloths, on the (correct) assumption that if it was covered it would be of value, probably perishable. One of the mates came up to me as I was walking a barge between some lighters and told me to bring a paper bag and follow him. I caught a temporary turn round a bollard to restrain the barge from blowing back where she had come from, fetched a paper bag from the cabin and went after him. Dark, quiet figures were clustered around the end of a sheeted lighter; someone had turned back a corner of the hatchcloth; one man was in the hold scooping up the contents into such containers as the others handed down to him. I took a look, and my clear soprano voice rang out over the otherwise hushed night: 'Oooooh, *sugar*!" It's a wonder I didn't get heaved straight into the oily waters of the dock! There was a united: "Sssssh", and no doubt some very black looks from those around me, and as soon as my paper bag had been filled I slipped away, much mortified.

Is there a statute of limitations in this country? I almost hesitate to mention another incident of larceny in which we were involved. This was also in post war years, when meat, among other comestibles, was strictly rationed. We were lying alongside a large cargo carrier in the King George V Dock waiting to transfer into her our freight of cement from the Medway. She must have been nearly empty. Our decks being almost flush with the water, her hull towered above quite twenty feet, and access to her topside was by way of one of those rope-sided, wooden-runged, ladders which it is impossible to climb with any degree of elegance. We were on deck clearing the gear out of the way preparatory to uncovering our hatchway when there was a hail from aloft at the ship's rail: "Ahoy, sailorman. 'Ware below!" And next moment something hurtled down and bounced on to the hatchway. It was a very small, very frozen lamb carcase.

Now, I know a skipper who would have tucked that lamb underneath one arm, climbed up the ship's ladder and over the rail, doffed his woolly hat to the tallyman on deck, and said politely: "Excuse me, I think you dropped this." But I'm afraid the moral fibre of my skipper was not always strong; in this case he was on to the prize in a flash, and we had it down in the cabin in two shakes of a — lamb's tail. Where to hide it, though, in case of search? Nowhere in its present shape, that was obvious. Imagine, please, trying to cut into pieces a solidly frozen lamb with the only tools to hand: a rather blunt bread knife and a carpenter's saw. We carried out the grizzly task on the cabin floor, sorely cramped for elbow room; hacked it into two shoulders and two legs and two rib sections (thanking Providence for sending it without a head) wrapped the pieces in newspaper and stowed them in odd corners in cupboards and lockers. The cabin was littered with chippings of fat and bone, which I swept up and burnt in the cabin stove. We had the most delicious chops, two *each*, for dinner the next day; but of course the meat pretty soon thawed, and to avoid sinful waste we gave a lot of it away. The skipper took a leg home. The illicit delights of stolen fruit were widely distributed, and on the premise that poached salmon tastes better than if lawfully hooked, that little lamb was much appreciated by all who had a portion.

Chapter Thirteen

I Board a Sinking Ship

IN the course of our life on the water we suffered surprisingly few personal mishaps. Once the skipper was sawing up a piece of heavy timber which he needed to mend a broken board in the ceiling of the *Dingle* when the saw slipped and ran across his thumb nail. After a gasp of pain, and a moment to recover, he just went on sawing (though I, standing by, was reduced to a quivering jelly of sympathy). There was only one occasion when I suffered a physical injury. We were lying at anchor about a mile above Brightlingsea in the *Dingle*, waiting for the tide to make up enough for us to get to Rowhedge to load sand. It was, as so often, in the middle of a dark night. Came the time to set off up the river, the engine started, the skipper and I commenced to heave up the anchor. The *Dingle* had a patent windlass, a narrow steel barrel with linked-shaped slots which gripped the chain as it came through the anchor snatch and directed it down the hawse-pipe into the chain locker. We never really knew what happened, but we think the chain must have come tight suddenly and a few links slipped back from the windlass causing the handle I was using to jump. It slammed across the bridge of my nose and into my spectacles, one lens of which cut into the eyebrow. I collapsed on to the deck, but was only unconscious for a moment or two. The skipper helped me to my feet and along the deck aft where I subsided, dazed, on the cabin top, — and in that state I remained while the skipper nipped below and brought up my eiderdown. He tucked this around me, then raced up forward and got the rest of the chain aboard and the anchor clear of the water.

The *Dingle* then proceeded at top speed to Rowhedge where there was nobody to be found at the wharf, as the loading people were still in their shed, it being not yet quite time for them to start work. So the skipper woke up everybody for five miles around with the ship's hooter and eventually people started to arrive, wanting to know what all the noise was about. An ambulance was called, and I was carried ashore (not without difficulty) and whisked off to hospital. I was deposited on an examination table in the usual pristine environment of the casualty ward, in my rough none-too-clean working clothes. I heard a female voice say: "She's still unconscious." At which I opened an eye (the other being swollen shut) and said: "No, I'm not" — which made the nurse and the doctor laugh. When they'd cleaned up my face, the doctor said cheerfully: "You've got a broken nose, look — " and he wiggled it gently which made my eyes water. I said anxiously: "I'm not really *crying*, it's just my eyes watering." He said he understood. Then he sewed my eyebrow up, and while he was doing that, to distract me he asked questions about barges and we went on to discuss music. He said he had a hi fi machine on which he spent all his spare cash. After tidying me up they announced they were going to keep me in until next day in case I'd got concussion, but I insisted that I had to get back to my ship, so they got an ambulance to take me back to Rowhedge and gave me a note to take to a hospital when we arrived at Rochester (which was the condition of my discharge).

Loading was finished by the time I got back to the wharf and someone had helped the skipper cover up. Away we went: as soon as we were clear of the Colne the skipper sent me down to my bunk where I stayed, thankfully, until we arrived at Rochester. By that time I'd recovered and was able to return to my normal work. The skipper had been alone at the wheel for eight hours; I repaid that debt some time later when he had a bad dose of 'flu and I too brought the barge from the Colne to Rochester in one unbroken watch.

As a professional breed, bargemen were perhaps not given to gushing friendliness, though they were instantly ready to give one another a hand when needed. As an example of this, we were drifting down the Swin one day in the motorless *Clara*, and the tide was running us close to a wrecked ship on the steep Barrow Sand whose masts had stood clear of the water for many years. The water was too deep here for us to anchor and there wasn't a breath of wind to help us sail clear. Luckily a sand barge was on its way down Swin astern of us and spotted our predicament; he came alongside, took a quick turn with a rope and managed to claw us off, only in the nick of time. He couldn't afford to tow us far, or he'd have missed his tide at Rowhedge, but he took us over to the Maplin side of the channel, well clear of danger, before letting us go once more.

Any bargeman, sailing or motoring, always gave a cheery "hello" wave to crews of other passing barges. It was a great guessing game whenever any small craft appeared over the horizon as to who it would be. I quickly came to recognise the identity of all sorts of vessels, sometimes by their general shape, or by a glimpse of a particular colour of livery; and there was one we always could name before the hull even cleared the horizon, because it was making such a heavy pall of exhaust smoke.

One day in fine weather we were bouncing down Swin in the *Dingle*, empty, bound for Brightlingsea — mid-day, a breeze easterly, enough to make the spray fly from our bow and cause rainbows, but not enough to produce waves of any size. We passed close by the Whitaker Beacon, at the mouth of the Burnham River, to cut off a corner en route for the Spitway. There was another barge out there which we recognised as the old *Lord Roberts*, obviously bound up to Rochford Mill, and wasn't she deep loaded! my skipper commented. We passed astern of her, about a quarter of a mile off, and someone appeared out of her wheelhouse and stood at the taffrail waving both arms over his head. Now, there is a subtle difference between a man casually waving a greeting from a wheelhouse window or an open doorway, and the same man coming right out on deck and waving both arms overhead. The latter signal positively indicates a need for communication — please come alongside. We altered course, and came close alongside, but not close enough to touch, slowing right down to maintain that position. The *Lord Roberts* was making only slow progress, wallowing heavily in the mild easterly swell. It was the young mate who had signalled to us, but now the skipper had come out of the wheelhouse to the quarterdeck and was shouting:

"Have you got a motor pump aboard? We're making water, and it's gaining on the pumps."

My skipper replied yes, we had a pump. It was down in the engineroom, and while I fetched it he sheered away from the other barge, made a complete turn and manoeuvred alongside again. By now my little motor pump was on deck together with a couple of lengths of hosepipe, the starting cord and a gallon can of petrol, and the *Dingle* was near enough to the *Lord Roberts* for me to pass the lot down to the man standing on her hatchway. My skipper shouted to him: "Do you want my mate to come aboard and assist?"

With every appearance of relief the man in the *Lord Roberts* nodded. My skipper told me he would put me aboard the stricken *Lord Roberts* to help them round to Rochford, while he continued on his own to Brightlingsea. I nipped down below to collect my jacket and some money to pay for a long train journey, then came back on deck, and while the skipper held the *Dingle* steady close by I jumped down from our deck on to the hatchway of the *Lord Roberts*. Then, with a wave of the hand, he headed off for the Spitway.

On board the *Lord Roberts* I set up the little motor pump on deck with the hosepipe leading down through the engineroom skylight into the black water which could be seen swirling sullenly, half way up the sides of the engine. Now there is an irrefutable and well-known truth about portable motor pumps. Under test they will respond instantly to the first flick of the starting cord and after a couple of convulsive gulps they will lift water up from one place and spit it out in neat pulses somewhere else. But, in cases of emergency, for which their acquisition at great expense is made, they back up, go all coy and refuse to start until the fiftieth tug of the cord, by which time your arm is nearly paralysed. The motor started, it's the pump that now refuses duty. So, you get a bucket of water and a jug and pour water down the short length of discharge hose in an effort to prime the pumping mechanism. I had gone through the ritual time and time again. My skipper was a model of patience, but even he became livid with rage when the pump refused to do its duty — despite at an earlier testing having instantly pumped like crazy.

Well, there aboard the *Lord Roberts* was I, secretly in a fever of worry, and very methodically I went through the motions of getting the pump set up. I drew a bucket of water and asked the mate to bring a jug; I stood the machine in a level, stable position on deck; I saw that the end of the hosepipe was well below the surface of the water in the engine room (but not so deep it could suck up muck); I wound the cord round the starter three times — and with metaphorical fingers crossed, gave it a powerful controlled heave. The motor started immediately. Without waiting to see if it would pump water unprimed, I poured half a bucket down the discharge pipe and stood back. There was a loud, choking cough from the pump, then black oily water came gushing out on to deck. What a relief! I could have jumped for joy, but of course I maintained a suitable decorum before the crew and pretended I wasn't at all surprised.

The barge's engine was also pumping away for all it was worth (which wasn't much) and they had a hand pump shipped, so while her skipper headed the barge up the Whitaker Channel the mate and I took turns at the handle.

This promising state of affairs lasted for about twenty minutes. Then the main engine died, and apart from the chunter of my little pump all was quiet. Three heads looked down through the engineroom skylight into stygian depths of blackness; the water had risen to cover the engine completely.

We were still a long way from land. The flood had just started to come, but the sands on both sides of the Whitaker were dry and the easterly wind was dead on our stern. At that time the *Lord Roberts* retained her mainmast with a leg o' mutton sail lashed tight against it. Her skipper for the moment appeared bemused, and stood there with a vacant look. I was in a somewhat delicate situation, being a mere mate, and a woman to boot, but after a few moments of silence I asked him, extremely humbly, if it wouldn't be possible to set the sail, and wouldn't the fair wind bring us into the shelter of the Crouch where we could run the barge on the shore? He looked at the sail very doubtfully and said he'd never unfurled it since taking charge of the *Lord Roberts*. Then, as the truth of the matter sunk in, he was galvanised into action, and threw off the sail's lashings to shake out the folds. The wind instantly filled the sail and the barge began to chuckle through the water; the skipper went back to the wheel and with steady streams of water coming from the motor pump and the hand pump, we made a slow but sure progress into the River Crouch. The water down below was still gaining on us, but nevertheless we were able to turn the corner into the Roach, some miles below the mill where the freight of wheat was bound, and a bit before high water the barge was beached in a convenient place where she would dry out as the tide left, thus enabling the water to be pumped clear.

As soon as she was comfortably settled the skipper put me ashore in the hope of getting a train for Brightlingsea. I sat on a bench on Rochford Station, blinking in the warm sunshine, thinking of my little adventure and wondering if the *Dingle* got safely to the loading wharf. Later that evening I joined her there. She had got loaded, but had missed her tide of course. So we lay alongside and left on the next flood.

Some of the wheat in the *Lord Roberts*' hold was spoiled by being soaked in salt water, but apparently the better part of it was saved due to our getting her beached in time. She was pumped out and then towed up to the mill for discharge. My skipper wrote to the barge's insurers and suggested that they might make a small award to me for my part in the rescue; they were good enough to present me with a gold wristwatch.

Chapter Fourteen

I Help to Build a Nuclear Power Station

NOWADAYS I rarely find myself within a hundred miles of the M2 road bridge over the Medway in Kent, or of the Bradwell Nuclear Power Station in the remote eastern corner of Essex, but when I do I smile to myself and am secretly proud to think that I helped to build those two monuments to twentieth century progress.

The *Dingle* was one of a constant stream of barges carrying ballast to the site of the new Medway bridge; it was a wild place to discharge a freight. Arrived at a point built out into the river so that a tall crane on top of one of the new bridge supports could unload a barge at any state of tide, we would tie the barge up as best we could with ropes round piles, and the crane grab would hurtle down from a tremendous height landing with a resounding bump on the pile of whatever we'd brought — time after time, non-stop, until we were empty. If there was time to get completely empty we did our own shovelling, otherwise we hurried away with a few yards left in the hold, which the grab couldn't scrape up, and another barge promptly took our place. We had no chance to go ashore; not that there was anything nearby to interest us, such as a grocery shop. If we needed provisions we dropped down to Rochester and lay there for an hour on a buoy.

Far more interesting were the weeks we spent supplying ballast for the foundations of the Nuclear Power Station at Bradwell on the south shore of the Blackwater Estuary. Part of the contract was offered to us and the price we did it for was about half that for carrying ballast to London. The contract called only for mixed ballast — the heaviest, ungraded ballast available, scooped up from the pits to be dumped straight into the barge, a mixture encompassing sand and small, medium and large gravel — right up to big irregularly shaped stones, practically rocks. I believe it weighed 30 cwt to the cubic yard. There was enough water for a loaded barge on what passed for a jetty at the building site at most states of tide, except for an hour each side of low water. The distance from the loading wharf was no more than ten miles, so a barge's running expenses were minimal. I don't think we were ever able to load, motor to Bradwell, unload and get back again to the loading berth all on the same tide, but we very nearly did. Weather was no problem; we barely touched the open sea, so we loaded our barge far deeper than when bound out for the Thames. Usually we didn't bother to put the hatches on, though there were a few occasions when we found her to be so deep loaded as to have water on deck (instead of the normal foot of side clear). At such times we did put the hatches on if there was any sort of popple in the estuary; we just couldn't afford to ship any extra weight of water in the hold. There was an occasion during a flat calm, with the sea like shot silk, when the skipper allowed them to put 200 yards of ballast into the *Dingle* — estimated 300 tons! I believe the ship would have split at the seams had she not been riveted throughout. Afloat, the water came three inches up the hatch coamings, but as I say it was a perfectly calm day, and we quickly covered the short distance from Colne to Bradwell. The skipper of another barge who saw us, later said we nearly gave him a heart attack, for the only parts of the *Dingle* showing above the surface were the wheelhouse and the mast. He must have thought we were a submarine.

*   *   *

All of that happened to me a relatively short time ago, but in a very different world. While we had the *Dingle* in the late fifties and early sixties a small revolution was taking place. We acquired an electronic depth sounder, a radio transmitter and an automatic steering device with controls, if required, at the end of a long lead which enabled a barge to be steered from right up for'ard. We also had a short-range walkie talkie system, so that I could speak to the skipper in the wheelhouse while standing up forward to keep a lookout in thick weather. These appliances changed working conditions on a small ship in a way not to be imagined by us only ten years earlier. But now, twenty years on, the world of barges and small ships has taken yet another course. Skippers and mates are required to be licensed; equipment such as lights, radios, and navigational aids, is governed by precise rules — made in Brussels. Going up the Thames today a skipper is required to call up succeeding stations on his radio, announcing his whereabouts, signing out of one area and into the next. When I was loose on the river, navigation was a continual science of cheating foul tides and taking the utmost advantage of fair ones; of crossing from one side to the other as the exigencies of the passage dictated, regardless of the ancient rule of keeping to starboard and the sensible practice of working inwards on the flood and outwards on the ebb. Up among the London bridges, little ships like us as well as big "flat-irons" (colliers that took coal to gas works and power stations) and tugs with long strings of lighters would all jostle about between the arches according to the state of tide and the headroom available. If a collier coming down empty was too high to get through the down arch he would have to take the up arch, but was expected to wait until the arch was clear of up going traffic. Did she heck! Might is right! It was more usually little 'uns like us who kept out of her way even though we were technically justified in claiming the arch.

Times have changed. Today the London river above Gravesend is almost empty of commercial traffic. Twenty short years ago it was so full of life. Fifty sailing barges which had their gear taken out of them and were fitted with engines in my day have been bought up by enthusiastic amateurs and restored to former glory — some returned to trade as trip boats, carrying all sorts from infants to plutocrats, around the bay and a little further.

Would they, I wonder, have given me a mate's certificate of competency had there been such things thirty years ago? I doubt it, since I was a mere female. Today, however, I'm told it isn't all that difficult for a girl to obtain a full blown master's certificate. Times, as I say, have changed.

F I N I S

Some notes on the history of my three barges

*T*HE Clara *was built in 1896 at Alfred White's Sittingbourne yard for Ambrose Ellis of Stanford le Hope in Essex, a wooden sailing barge of 60 tons Register. She cost £700.*

In the year of her launch she competed successfully in the Medway sailing barge match, the winner in her class. (Earlier she had been beaten into second place in the Thames match by the celebrated flyer Haughty Belle — by a mere ten minutes.)

From 1909 until 1914 the Clara was occupied exclusively with the work of Meeson the miller of Battlesbridge, generally carrying corn in 120 ton parcels between London docks and the River Crouch. She is remembered for making several crossings to the Continent during the First World War. Once (at Christmas 1917) she got into trouble off Broadstairs while on passage to Calais, lost her anchor and had to be helped into Ramsgate by some fishermen.

The Clara joined the Colchester fleet of Francis & Gilders at some stage in the early 1930s and remained under that flag for twenty years until purchased by Richard Banyard jnr. of Little Totham, Essex, and put to work on his own account. After severe damage sustained in the Thames in 1954 the Clara was taken to Hampton to be used as the headquarters of a Sea Scout troop. She was finally broken up in 1968.

*   *   *

The Olive May was launched in 1920 — one of the very few sailing barges designed for auxiliary power. Her builders were the respected firm of Wills & Packham at Sittingbourne; but Captain Arthur Wenben, one of several part-owners, had taken a hand in her design. She was not the success he had hoped for: her registered tonnage, by only a small margin, placed her in too high a category for vessels of her class, and port and river dues were crippling; her hold was too deep for places where there was no crane for loading and

93

discharging; her draught too great for many of the smaller wharves except at spring tides.

Early in her career the Olive May *earned the name of an unlucky ship, and through half-a-century of trading she maintained a bad reputation. She was one of the largest wooden sailing barges ever built, measuring in length 98 feet and across the beam 23 feet. Her cargo hold was eight feet deep; her official load-line capacity was in the region of 265 tons (but there are many known occasions when she carried loads of 300 tons and more).*

When Captain Wenben died of a heart attack in 1932, the barge passed into the ownership of Samuel West of Gravesend. Her original auxiliary engine (a Vickers-Petter semi-diesel of 76 h.p.) was replaced by a 150 h.p. Crossley model DR6, arranged for compressed-air starting and direct drive to the shaft, the latter involving the notable inconvenience of having to stop and re-start the engine each time a shift from "ahead" to "astern" was required. When attempting to manoeuvre in close quarters, or running slowly (when the Crossley tended to stall), no small strain was placed on the engineroom's limited supply of compressed air!

She was sent up to the Clyde to work for the Royal Navy during the Second World War, one of a number of Thames barges so directed, afterwards resuming her pre-war career of "long-haul" coasting. Her sailing gear had already been discarded in 1938; it was reinstated in some modified form after Wests disposed of her to a private owner at the end of the 1960s. She survives today as a yacht-barge.

*   *   *

The X-lighters (or "beetles" as they were colloquially termed) were all built in 1915 or 1916 for the Dardanelles invasion. The Dingle *was a "beetle" barge; the Royal Navy knew her as X-90; she was one of the first batch of 200, and built at the Caledon Yard in Dundee.*

Her class (there were two classes) measured 105 feet 6 inches in length and 21 feet across the beam. She was fitted originally with a 50 h.p. Bolinder hot-bulb oil engine. Nobody knows whether the Dingle *actually got out to the Dardanelles, though many of her sisters did — and returned home to work in peace (and peaceably in a later war) for what will soon be seven decades.*

After the Armistice many "beetles" were sold off to civilian firms and transformed into commercial motor-barges. A few became water and fuel tankers in the River; most embarked on the infinitely harder life of coastwise cargo carriers; many have long exceeded the allotted span as ballastmen like my own Dingle; *three survive to this day in the Colne sand work, though in a new and unrecognisable guise — the* Colin P., *the* Sidney P., *and the* Peter P. *— rebuilt in 1963, losing the old characteristic spoon-bow; the* Beam *still loads general cargo; there may be others yet.*

The loss in February 1962 of a "beetle" barge (the Delce), *with skipper and mate, caused a public outcry which resulted in a strict enforcement of loading regulations and sea-going limits. Earlier another "beetle" working sand and ballast (the* Alpheus) *had been lost with all hands. It was a hard trade, of which the designer of the X-lighters can never have dreamed; they served it well, and as a fleet long outlived all other veterans of that first war.*